"On these pages it is clear that we are wounded healers, that the path to God is one of downward mobility, and that all the ground is level at the foot of the cross."
—Shane Claiborne, author, activist, and director of Red Letter Christians

"This is the story we've never really heard told in the Church. It's inconvenient and necessary, hopeful and unflinching, humble and wry; as ferocious as love."
—Sarah Bessey, author of *Jesus Feminist* and *Out of Sorts: Making Peace with an Evolving Faith*

"Mayfield's daring prose pulls us into the poetics, the adventure, the ecology, and the anguish of being a true neighbor today."
—Chris Hoke, author of *Wanted: A Spiritual Pursuit Through Jail, Among Outlaws, and Across Borders*

"I cannot get enough of D. L. Mayfield's rich language, vivid storytelling, and nuanced perspective on faith, poverty, and the 'ministry of cake,' which has left me aching for the world she inhabits and the God she loves."
—Micha Boyett, author of *Found: A Story of Questions, Grace, and Everyday Prayer*

"In a season of such great fear of 'the other,' Mayfield's observations and exhortations are timely. Her heart is huge, her questions important, and her lovely prose pierced my soul."
—Jeff Chu, author of *Does Jesus Really Love Me?*

"*Assimilate or Go Home* is a book I will reach for again and again, not just for its pitch-perfect storytelling or its stripped-down theology, but because it's a postcard of where I've been, where I'm headed, and the innumerable times I will circle back, begin again, and find myself loved."

—Shannan Martin, author of *Falling Free: Rescued from the Life I Always Wanted*

"*Assimilate or Go Home* is the least American book about Christianity I've read by an American evangelical. Like the gospels, it foregrounds the troubles of human frailty, of pain, of not-knowing. Mayfield suggests perhaps we can replace power with an imperfect attempt at love."

—Kyle Minor, author of *Praying Drunk*

"Mayfield's voice aches like a psalmist's; it sings out like the prophets of old. This book is ancient wisdom, distilled from the daily grind, rendered in the vernacular of American life."

—Jonathan Wilson-Hartgrove, author of *Strangers at My Door*

"Mayfield pulls back the curtain on her life in the refugee community. The harsh reality of life lived purposefully in the margins reveals the raw, terrifying beauty of her innate belovedness."

—Addie Zierman, author of *When We Were on Fire* and *Night Driving*

"*Assimilate or Go Home* is among the most refreshing books I have read in years: funny, wise, and convicting."

—Matthew Soerens, U.S. Director of Church Mobilization at World Relief and coauthor of *Seeking Refuge*

ASSIMILATE
or
GO HOME

Notes from a Failed Missionary
on Rediscovering Faith

D. L. Mayfield

HarperOne
An Imprint of HarperCollins*Publishers*

HarperOne

HarperCollins books may be purchased for educational, business,
or sales promotional use. For information, please email the Special Markets Department at SPsales@harpercollins.com.

Originally published as Assimilate or Go Home in the United
States of America in 2016 by HarperCollins.

First HarperOne paperback published

FIRST EDITION

Library of Congress Cataloging-in-Publication Data

Names: Mayfield, Danielle L., author.
Title: Assimilate or go home : notes from a failed missionary on
    rediscovering faith / Danielle L. Mayfield.
Description: FIRST EDITION. | San Francisco : HarperOne, 2016.
Identifiers: LCCN 2016006050 (print) | LCCN 2016018858 (ebook)
| ISBN 9780062388803 (pbk.) | ISBN 9780062388810 (ebook)
Subjects: LCSH: Mayfield, Danielle L. | Church work with
refugees--United States. | Evangelistic work--United States.
Classification: LCC BV4466 .M39 2016 (print) | LCC BV4466
(ebook) | DDC 266.0092 [B] --dc23
LC record available at https://lccn.loc.gov/2016006050

Designed by Joan Olson

16 17 18 19 20   RRD(H)   10 9 8 7 6 5 4 3 2 1

Isn't the twentieth century the age of the expatriate, the refugee, the stateless—and the wanderer?

—Elie Wiesel

Contents

Author's Note

The names have been changed to protect the privacy of individuals in this book, but the stories are as true as my recollections allow. Writing about cultures and experiences that are so vastly different from my own, primarily within communities where there is a lack of literacy skills, adds another wrinkle to this task of wanting to be emotionally and ethically honest. I have tried my best to honor my friends and neighbors while still being true to what I saw and felt.

I was trying to explain to my young friends, Saida and Khadija, that I had written a book and that they were a big part of it. I felt nervous and stammered as I tried to explain what that meant, and I waited for a response. The girls, home from a tiring day of high school, were lounging on the couches in their living room, fiddling on phones and computers. "You wrote a book?" Khadija asked, not sounding that interested. "I knew you were a writer, but I didn't know that you wrote books." I told her that, yes, I wrote a book; it was about the time that I met them and how they changed my life. How their family in-troduced me to the realities of what it means to be a refugee in

America and how hard it can be. How they taught me so much about my own country and how they taught me so much about God. Finally, I trailed off. "Really," I said, "the book is about how you changed my life." Saida and Khadija both looked at me for a moment, and then looked at each other. "Of course we did," said Saida, and they went back to checking Facebook.

This book is for them. I can't wait until the day when they write down their own stories, for they will change us all.

Preface: Stateless Wanderers

"Love in action is harsh and dreadful compared to love in dreams."

— DOROTHY DAY, QUOTING DOSTOYEVSKY

Several years ago I showed *The Jesus Film* to an apartment packed with devout Muslims. I had ordered the VHS from a special minister-to-Muslims website (it was pretty old school—hence, the VHS). The viewers were Somali Bantu, recently arrived from decades spent languishing in a refugee camp. I was the earnest young volunteer with English language skills and free time to burn. The apartment was small, hot, and musty, smelling like close proximity and an easy community that I longed to be a part of.

I was nineteen years old, and I wanted to be a missionary.

The film was rather artlessly subtitled in Somali, and I didn't find out until later that my friends spoke a different, less well-known language. But still, they watched, patient with me and my strange film. I assumed it would translate well due to its color and drama, the histrionic and over-the-top filming, the copious close-up shots of weeping, strained faces. Combined with the soap-opera lighting, it was rather like a Bollywood film with none of the song-and-dance numbers. My friends watched patiently up until the pivotal crucifixion scene. At that moment, people began to busy themselves, picking up plates and chatting with each other, turning their gaze from the television set. I grew annoyed as the very narrative of my childhood was being ignored. I myself had been inflicted with the agony of watching a bad actor writhe around on a crucifix to somber and fuzzed-out music many, many times, and it had meant something to me. It wasn't until (spoiler alert!) Jesus appeared as his risen self, beatific and with beautiful, soft hair, that my friends turned their attention back to the film.

After it was over, everybody had to discuss it. I had no idea what they were saying, but I could tell it was passionate. The men did most of the arguing, but the women held their own, too. The kids, and there were a veritable sea of them in the apartment, clung to skirts and wiped their noses and leaned into one another, eyes wide and yet sleepy. Ali, the elder of the group, waved a hand at me. In his grand, broken English, he gave me their verdict. "Jesus," he said, holding the palm of his hand straight out in front of him, "is here."

"But Muhammad," he looked at me intently, for full effect, "is here." And with that, he moved his hand up by his head.

And that was that.

We never spoke of the film again, and I felt almost relieved. I had grown up wanting to be a missionary all my life, but when faced with a "real" mission field, I felt overwhelmed by the burden of proselytizing. I went to conferences and Bible studies and even majored in intercultural studies (which was evangelical code for missions), but nothing I learned seemed applicable when real people were in front of me, drinking chai and discussing my pasty appearance. *The Jesus Film* was a cop-out for me, a way to feel like the missionary I wanted to be but without any of the hard work of explaining the four spiritual laws.

Looking back on the experience, I see that as we were watching the film together, the heavy yoke of my desire to convert others began to slip off my shoulders. As I relaxed onto the couch and into a culture that felt as removed from my own as I could get, it became clear this wasn't going to work, yet I still felt happy. I sat on the couch and listened to the rhythms of a different language while children perched on either side of me and marveled at my short blond hair, caressing it with their fingers. And for the first time in a long while, I felt at rest. A tiny bit of their community had been passed on to me.

Suffice it to say, there were no conversions that night. To this day, more than a decade later, I still have not converted one single Muslim; I have not changed the minds of any of my friends. I am pretty much the worst missionary ever, for reasons quite varied.

I did not know how to express it, but in many ways I used to think of myself as a displaced person, longing for a home. I was raised a devout, conservative Christian, intent on saving the lives of everyone else. The world around me thought me strange and religious, a fundamentalist missionary. But I couldn't let go of my longing to make the world a better place. Long ago, it seemed, I had been ruined for the ordinary. Outside of religious circles, I learned to be quiet, to laugh at the jokes I didn't understand, to downplay my past and my future, and to focus so relentlessly on the present so that people would stop giving me funny looks. There was no place that I felt at home.

And then I met them, people who I thought I could be of use to. God had sent me a sign from the sky, conveniently dropping off a group of Muslims (from Africa!) into my very own backyard.

Slowly, I started to enter more fully into the world of my

refugee friends. As the days and months blended into years, I experienced strange paradoxes. The more I failed to communicate the love of God to my friends, the more I experienced it for myself. The more overwhelmed I felt as I became involved in the myriad of problems facing my friends who experience poverty in America, the less pressure I felt to attain success or wealth or prestige. And the more my world started to expand at my periphery, the more it became clear that life was more beautiful and more terrible than I had been told. The differences, although real, started to blur together a bit. Muslim, Christian, Somali, American. We were being told to assimilate or go home, but we couldn't do either.

Over the years I learned about the cycles that refugees go through as they learn to acclimate to their new homes and lives. There are four general stages: anticipation and excitement, reality setting in, depression and culture shock, and stabilization. With the first stage, many people experience the unbearable weight of dreams of the good life, fixating on being free from worry and pain and sickness and death. Once their feet are on the ground, many refugees experience a brief period of bliss, followed closely by the difficulties of adjustment—which is when reality sets in. This is followed by profound culture shock, when the traumas of resettlement start to show themselves in multiple ways, including depression and anxiety. Finally, many (but not all) refugees come to some degree of acceptance of their new life, stabilizing and finding ways to cope and even thrive in the midst of grief and homesickness. For many, if not all, displaced persons, however, this resettlement cycle is neither static nor a linear journey—individuals can move up and down the scale, taking steps forward only to be slammed back into square one.

Anticipation, reality, depression, acceptance. The resettlement cycle is a loose, fluid look at how so many in our world are being asked to envision and forge new lives for themselves, and what a rocky journey it can be. While I am not a refugee—and want to make clear that my experience pales in every way compared to the global refugee crisis we are currently experiencing—I still find myself drawn to this cycle, and I can see evidence of it in my own life. There was and is something to the emotional arc that connected with me, the process of leaving the safety and security of my background and religion and being launched into the wilder territory of discovering the kingdom of God.

Each chapter in this book takes one stage and presents a collection of essays that speak to my experience—learning that it was never my job to save, or convert, but rather to simply show up and believe. My own days of anticipation and excitement were filled with thoughts of converts and saving all the people. I quickly realized, however, how complicated both life and God are, and I started to become dissatisfied with easy solutions and my own role in them. From there, as I descended into the suffering that the poor in America face, all of the questions I had about God shimmered to the surface, and I was forced to confront whether or not I believed the good news was actually good at all. And lastly, while I have not fully arrived, I eventually discovered that I am more loved by God than I could have possibly believed, even in the midst of great failure.

The essays in this book are not necessarily chronological, but instead paint a picture of my life as I've come to discover it. In this new land I now live in, even the most far-off wanderers find a place. Here, everything is upside down, completely opposite from what we have been sold all along. I started to read the

scriptures with new eyes, informed by the people who wrote
the Bible and the people to whom it was written—the people at
the margins of society, the stateless wanderers of the earth. And
it was so much better than I could have believed. The blessings of Jesus were to be found in the most unexpected places,
for those with the eyes to see them. The kingdom is real, alive,
and changing everything—liberating, setting free, healing, and
preaching news that is truly good in the here and now.

This book is the story of how I began to see glimpses of that
good kingdom. It is also the story of how I started off wanting
to convert everyone around me and instead found myself blessed
by the surprising relationships that ensued when I started to
place myself in the communities of people Jesus always said he
would be found in.

This is the story of how I wandered into the upside-down
kingdom, of how I was converted and am still being converted
every day.

But really, it's the story of how I failed miserably, and what
a good thing that turned out to be.

1

Anticipation and Excitement

Light and Dark

I can still remember the exact day when everything changed.

It was Christmas, the season for church choirs and sparkling lights and crisp air and the glorious feeling of being so connected to the stars and to the birth of new things for the world, the season I longed for all year. I had found myself at a sprawling farmhouse in the countryside outside of Portland, Oregon, the wind blowing a terrible cold into my bones. A church friend told me she was throwing a Christmas party for some recently arrived African refugees and asked if I wanted to come help out.

'Twas the season after all, and I amiably told her I would come. I showed up at my friend Jan's house, past the suburbs to the rolling fields. I stepped out of the car and shivered, looked around. There was no snow on the ground, but the wind was chilly and the temperature near freezing. I immediately noticed two dozen or so strange figures dotting the pastoral landscape: women in billowing thin cloaks that were brightly colored, men in loose button-up shirts and trousers wearing tiny hats on their heads. And children, wiry, compact, and brown, dressed in shorts and sandals, as unprepared for winter as one could possibly be. After a moment or two to get over the shock of it all, I snapped into missionary mode: bustling about, shaking hands, introducing myself, being the welcoming fool. The adults seemed wary, but the kids ate up the attention.

Some of the children ran around the small playground,

yelping with joy. Others gazed rapturously at the cows and horses scattered around in nearby pastures. And still other children huddled together in groups by the swing set, shivering. It was difficult to tell the gender of many of them, as they all had identical buzz cuts (due to an outbreak of lice, we later found out) and greatly ill-fitting and outdated clothing.

It was a shock, this scene within a scene. I felt as though I had fallen into the kind of advertisement where they blindside you with pictures of malnourished children gazing piteously at the camera, the kind of ad where they ask you for money, where they kick you in the gut. But I wasn't looking at a glossy advertisement, and I didn't know what I was being asked to do; I was at my friend's house, surrounded by people for whom I had no context, except to see them as victims of their own poverty. My memories of this day are clouded by the assumptions I brought with me, a swirling mix of media images about Africa, a fluttering excitement over exoticness, a desire to bridge cultural differences, and the general urge one gets around the holidays to help those who are in need.

Eventually, everyone was ushered in for a meal. Confusion ensued (many of the refugees had never used Western utensils before, we inadvertently offended by not offering food to the men first, etc.). The adults halfheartedly picked at the pasta with red sauce. The bread was devoured in seconds. The salad stood alone and untouched.

My friend Jan, whose parents owned the farm, circled us all into the living room and had her dad read the nativity story from the book of Matthew. A large, jolly man with a successful family medical practice, he read the story like he had probably done every year: authoritatively, boomingly, reenacting the scene (complete with voice changes) for the little ones. I vaguely remember trying to act out the nativity scene: there was a lot of shrieking and kids rolling around on the floor. We sang

Christmas carols for a while, but then somebody brought out a couple of hand drums and our visitors took over, playing their traditional songs for us.

I have little to no memory of the adults in the room. My gaze fixated helplessly on the children, who appeared intent on the story, but more likely than not were just simply happy to be warm and full of bread. Perfectly happy like only children can be, they sprawled out on carpets, while their parents sat stiff in the folding chairs.

A little girl around four years old crawled into my lap and promptly fell asleep. Her family (there were four separate Somali Bantu families at the Christmas party that day, although it would take me months to be able to sort them out) had only been in America for three days. Three days? I felt like the luckiest soul in the world to be the first American to hold her, that dusty and cold and beautiful child. When she peed on me, supremely comfortable in her sleep, I was shocked to find myself suppressing a smile of joy.

I felt at home here. I was a lost and aimless college student, a girl with missionary dreams in a homogenous town, a student at a theologically conservative Bible college. But here I was, sitting with people with foreign, traumatic backgrounds. I was surrounded by Muslims, women with head scarves, the scent of ginger clinging to the skirts all around me. And yet I was also inside a warm farmhouse where the story of Jesus and his humble origins had just been preached. The juxtaposition delighted me, the entire day and the scenario a singular experience that only I could truly appreciate. Cradling that little girl in my lap, soaked in piss and singing Christmas carols, I knew I could be of use to these newly arrived refugees, that I could do some tangible good in this world. It was an intoxicating feeling.

And, as it turns out, rather fleeting. I would be chasing these highs for the next several years of my life, but it would always leave me unsatisfied—until I stopped seeing people like an advertisement for help, when I stopped viewing myself as the generous benefactor, the Santa Claus that decided who had been good or naughty, who was worthy of help or not. It would take many years to get this out of my skin, and still it is not completely gone.

I did not know then what I know now; I can only hope that I continue to learn. Whatever the case, at that moment I knew I had found my world within worlds that cold December day. I could feel the doors of my life opening wider, letting in others who were so different from me, letting in the spirit of God. I had found people as different from me as the night is from the day. What I didn't know then was that the seeds of my own blindness were orchestrating my thoughts. For, of course, in viewing our differences, I thought I was the sun and they were the darkness.

I signed up to volunteer with the refugees the next day. It was the day that changed everything because it was the day my friendship with the poor started. And just like the Bible said, it was the poor, the sick, and the sad who would be blessed in the kingdom of God—and they would be the ones who revealed it to me.

O, Pioneers

The other day I was in a famous art gallery, where one of the photographs caught my attention. It was a small black-and-white image of a tree, willowy branches obscuring the lower left of the frame, a snapshot of a hot and still summer night. I read the plaque to the right, which described the photographer and how she used her pictures to grapple with her past, how she used her art to come to terms with the South where she grew up. I looked at that picture of the tree, and I experienced a flash of jealousy. I was envious that the photographer—who I imagined to be young and white, just like me—had such a tangible place to struggle with, a land still chock-full of confederate flags and weeping willows where nooses once hung. She was from a place, more for worse than for better, with a history that no one could dare forget. I myself wished I had a geography to praise and to blame. *I wish I was from someplace,* I thought.

It was then that I realized that perhaps this was my identity, a key to what made me tick. I was from everywhere and nowhere at the same time. I was, and remain to this day, a pioneer child, raised in a crash of western states—California, Oregon, Wyoming, Alaska—always on the move, always looking for the next good thing. I never had one patch of earth to claim. I had no place to call home.

I grew up a nomad, and I thought it was normal. My father was brilliant and goofy and on track to be a doctor when he dedicated his life to Jesus the summer he was a senior in high school. His father, an engineer for NASA, was deeply displeased. My dad went to a small Bible college in central California and hung out with the other smart, nerdy, gap-toothed guys who listened to the Beatles and the Beach Boys and learned how to make God rational and logical and convey that truth to others.

It was there, at Bible college, that he met my mom, a demure and beautiful sun-kissed girl from Kansas. Inside, however, she was a wild child, recently born-again and fresh off of stints of homelessness, heroin, and being forced to grow up way too soon. They fell in love, got married, and started what would become a decades-long cycle of packing up beaten-down cars with all of their earthly possessions, caravanning from church to church, unpacking and having babies, and then doing it all over again a few years later. They both came from immigrants, hardy folk with complicated relationships to the land and to others. And they both took unexpected paths through life, raising us to do the same.

My family moved around constantly, exploring the wilderness of the unknown, my dad taking jobs working with small churches and building them up. There were dusty pews and scraping folding chairs in gymnasiums, Bible studies and youth groups and potlucks. There were minor and major crises to be solved, always a parishioner upset about something, always a neighborhood outreach to get involved in. After a few years, the itch would start, the boxes would come out, and we would be off to another state, another town, and we would do it all over again.

The peak of our wandering ways came when I was eight years old and my parents sold our house in Alaska and put all of our belongings in storage. They then bought an old camper van and an atlas and set off to cover as much of the country as possible. They were harried souls, longing for a respite from pastoring, from catering to the already saved, and we found a bit of peace and quiet with our months on the road.

I remember it as a mostly sweet, carefree time. I loved that old camper, loved living so tight and calm with my family surrounding me, my two sisters and I watching the sunsets from the bed on top of the cab. But I was still attuned to what little I knew of the darker aspects of our life choices. "We're homeless now," my parents would laugh, joking with the friends that we saw along the way. Always a sober child, the humor was lost on me. While everyone laughed, I would stand apart—quiet, wondering, and worrying. I was old enough to know that one needed jobs and a stable place in order to raise a family. My sisters, one older, one younger, were not bothered like I was that we were living out of a car. They embraced every element of the grand adventure we were in, enjoying the differences while I nurtured the secret shame of thinking us poor, of not having the same options as our friends.

When I was a child I thought about poverty constantly, believing that my family was always one step away from the poorhouse that I was always reading about in my middle-grade novels. I was young but knew we were just one bad job away from living in our car for good. I developed a sense of watchfulness; I became an uneasy observer of all that I did not understand. I grew up invisible, because I wanted to be. Surrounded on either side by boisterous sisters, a strong mother, a preacher father, I was the quiet one, shy and stubborn and deeply concerned with the inequalities in my own small world. My mind was a sponge, eager to learn how to be right, how to set things right.

Eventually, our familial rootless and weightless ways became a source of pride. We made our own country, wherever we went. It was always presented as a great adventure, and I never questioned that it wasn't. My mother homeschooled us, let us pick what we were interested in, and then we were off and running until our minds were full. Our days were spent wandering in fields and backyards, jumping on trampolines and swinging in hammocks. In the mornings we did our chores and then sat together on the couch and read our Bibles, my mother and my two sisters and I. I learned to find things in the scriptures, I learned to listen, I learned that I very much wanted to be good. This is the mixture you get when you are raised on the body and the blood of Christ from a very young age. You can get so much of the benefits: a stable, loving family, the unshakable belief that you are known by God, the coloring books of a Jesus who adores the little children. But it can also become a way to navigate the world, without anyone ever explicitly telling you so: to become good at religion, quick at all the right answers, will ensure a better life. It will mean that God loves you, that God goes with you in all of your journeys, that there is a formula for blessing just waiting to be grasped.

The shifting sands of geography in my past do not photograph as well as a weeping willow, but if I squint, I can see all of the same themes. I see itchy feet, the privilege of being able to pick up and move on with the wind, the freedom of chosen statelessness. I see how the pioneer spirit is strong within me, the desire to experience the wonder of the next great adventure, the urge to chronicle all the new frontiers I experience. I see how quick I am to commandeer a situation, to domesticate it, to run roughshod over those who have been here longer. I also see how I have routinely given up so much to keep my pack light, but this in its own way has been both a blessing and a curse. To be forever a pioneer, forever a self-identified wanderer, is to never take responsibility for how deeply the myths of the American Dream can get into your blood.

I grew up loved and cherished and transient. And I grew up believing these myths of manifest destiny and exceptionalism, the idea that I could do or be anything that I ever dreamed of, and assumed it was true of everyone else if they only did right and tried hard. I grew up a pioneer, courageous and flawed, relentlessly propelled forward by a desire to obey God and to share his love for the world. I always thought this would take me to the wildest places I could imagine—post-Communist Russia, sub-Saharan Africa, a tiny village in India—but I never conceived that I would ever be asked to stay put. It never entered my mind that one day I would grow up. I never thought I would settle down, that I would always be looking for a strange new world to encounter. And I ended up finding it, in the most unlikely of places. I found my belonging among those who truly had no home to go back to, and they taught me more than I ever wanted to know about the land of the free, the brave, the pioneers.

Vacation Bible Schools

That first Christmas, when that little girl crawled into my lap and fell asleep, I knew I needed to be involved in some way with this refugee community. As I began to volunteer with the families, helping them acclimate to America in whatever ways I could, I was drawn deeper and deeper into their community, which continually shed light on my own culture. A few years into my work living and working among the Somali Bantu refugees, I took a bunch of the kids to a Vacation Bible School, a staple of the churches I grew up in. That summer was the second one most of the Somali Bantu kids had spent in America, and they were languishing in the heat and lack of supervision that summer brings.

After years of moving around, my dad had settled into a large, successful megachurch in the suburbs of Portland, Oregon. Hundreds of kids crammed into a beautiful auditorium filled with good-natured volunteers running around trying to stop children from killing each other. The theme of the week was "The Serengeti," and the whole place was decked out with African-themed images (what this had to do with the Bible, or Jesus, I will never know). I had brought a van full of kids from the apartment complex, and they stared in silent amazement at all the large cutouts of giraffes and elephants decorating the stage. They clapped their hands and screamed along to the songs, they listened patiently to the Bible story of the day, they made their crafts and ate their snacks with gusto. I was so proud, so self-congratulatory for being a good missionary and bringing these kids to the church. And then, as I was herding the refugee kids toward the water fountains, I overhead a small child talking to a volunteer. "Oh!" he said joyously, "they brought us kids from the Serengeti!" Several children turned and pointed at me and my group, and I felt my face begin to flush as I realized *the church kids thought the refugee kids were props.*

I wanted to self-righteously shake my finger and rant about "othering" people, but I was supposed to be the exemplary volunteer. So instead I made sure all the kids I brought got their snacks and sat at their table, and I glared at everyone around me. I felt smug, secure in my own saintliness as I bustled around my group of exotics, the only diverse kids in the large, pale bunch. I drove all the kids home, but decided not to bring them the next night. How sad, I thought woefully, that not everyone could be as enlightened as me—could love their poor neighbors as well, could be as effective an arm and leg of Christ. Because look at me! Driving a van full of children born into poverty and desperation, children who had never sung songs about hippos and Jesus before!

I drove all the kids home, confident in my own goodness. As it turns out, I also believed that my refugee friends were a sort of prop: nominal, one-dimensional stories in the great saga of my own life. When I finally started to believe the opposite, to see them as complex, flesh-and-blood people, everything got much, much harder.

And my view of myself was irrevocably changed.

This wasn't my first run-around with a VBS. As a child, I loved Vacation Bible School time. There was something magical about the familiar church being transformed into a place for neighborhood children, when the ranks of my Sunday school class swelled with kids I didn't know. When I was nine, my family living in a small town in Wyoming, our 1960s-era church was transformed into the isle of Patmos, the place where the apostle John wrote his fantastical book of the end times. I don't recall anything about the curriculum (and that is saying something, since it was based on the book of Revelation). Instead, I marveled at the glassy blue sea (paper, taped down on the carpet), the fake palm trees surrounding the beige walls, the way we all had to huddle together on the island, to hear the words of the Lord, to sing our songs in solidarity, to be a part of something special and different and designed just for us. I felt like I had been to an island, that week. In a way, it was a vacation for me, a respite from the windy, dusty town where we had been planted.

When I was in high school, living in central Oregon, the youth group kids and I would all pile into vans, tumbling together with sleeping bags and backpacks, giddy on hormones and the sense that we were doing something grown-up and important, traveling from the windy, high desert plains of central Oregon to the great big city of Portland, pressing our faces to the windows to catch a sight of urbanity that was mostly lost on us. Young, unfettered by the world, we did not worry about things like traffic or directions or plans. We were sheep; clamoring, good-hearted, incredibly annoying sheep. We were there to find some more little lambs, to herd them into the pasture, to bring them into the fold. We were there to do our own version of Vacation Bible School with inner-city children.

On the first trip I was fifteen, both opinionated and shy, missionary zeal already burning in my heart, fear freezing my lips. My small, rural youth group got connected to an inner-city church, and we came with all our baggage to help on our summer vacation. While others went to Mexico to party or California to see grandparents, we slept in the church sanctuary on the floor and ate peanut butter sandwiches. For the first few days we would go out and canvass the neighborhood where we were going to set up our own Vacation Bible School, here called a Five Day Club so as to not attract so much suspicion to the word "Bible." Five Day Clubs were weeklong events where kids would come, sing songs, and learn about Jesus. Sometimes there were crafts involved, or puppets, or people dressed up in mascot costumes. There were always snacks. Always. The first day our van dropped us off at an apartment complex, big and dark green, looming over us kids from the country. We were paired off, handed a stack of flyers, and commissioned to go and knock on doors, inviting children to attend our club, which was to start the next day.

The majority of doors remained closed to us, and our fearful hearts rejoiced just a little that we didn't have to speak just yet, feeling the full weight of our words. This was us, evangelizing. This was us, knocking tentatively, unprepared for when someone would let us into their lives.

When they did, I was taken into a world I didn't know existed. If the door opened to us at all, it was usually by a small child, three or four or five years old. In my memory, although this could not possibly be true, all of the children in the complex were small, silent, and staring at us giant teenagers. They squinted at us against the summer sun, saying nothing. We stammered, asked for a parent to talk to. The door would shut, we would hear conversations in languages we didn't recognize, and then minutes later the door would open. A mother, interrupted from the process of cooking the day's food, would come to the entryway, staring at the two white girls at her door. We would explain why we were there and shove the flyers into hands of people who couldn't read them. Blinking ensued, all around. My fellow evangelist and I were taken aback. We were expecting to knock on doors and find people different from us, of course. We were just too young to understand how enormous those differences could be, to be aware of all the worlds within the American landscape. Shaking it off, we realized we needed to get on with our mission.

We resorted to repeating the words "tomorrow, tomorrow, tomorrow. Food, games, tomorrow," gesturing toward the nearby field and basketball court where we were going to bring the Truth to this apartment complex. We got a few nods of assent, watched the doors close to us again. I only saw glimpses into the apartments, but it was enough for me to know the way I had been living my life was so different from how these people were living theirs. And even through all of my fear and giddiness and my firm belief in the importance of evangelism, I realized more than anything—I wanted to live here, in the midst of them. I wanted to understand where they had come from, the ways they lived their lives. I wanted to eat their food and see if I could get anyone to laugh. I wanted to understand this place, this apartment complex that was a place itself inside a city that could care less; I wanted to escape and be changed by the people who were to me as exotic as a palm tree, a man-made island in the midst of my long blue sea of a life. I was a child of heart and mind, but a few apartment doors had been opened up to me. My life seemed so much brighter by comparison now that I had seen such a small piece of the differences there were to experience.

Many of the kids did come to our Five Day Club, sitting quiet and withdrawn in the brown August grass, sniffling occasionally into their sleeves. My fellow volunteers and I wore zany costumes and told Bible stories and the children sat and watched us calmly, detached from the mania. Most of them did not deign to smile, let alone laugh. We made bracelets and ate our orange slices and drank our juice boxes in the sunshine, the older kids ushering the younger ones around, making sure to procure food for the littlest ones first, the ones who stared at us. I would later find out they were tribal clans from Southeast Asia with a story unique yet so similar to many around the world: sent to refugee camps after their communities had been slaughtered, put on planes to places like Portland and given eight months of assistance to get on their feet. I would read later, much later in my life, scholarly accounts describing the difficulty refugees can experience while adjusting to life in the Western world. And I would be transported back to the circle of us sitting crisscross applesauce, teaching happy little songs about Jesus to little children who were just barely treading water.

We didn't know any of this. In the blessed ways of teenagers, we were too self-absorbed to notice any discomfort, any communication issues due to lack of language. We didn't understand the sickness rampant in the community, the households that could not afford heat for the coming winter. We didn't know about the cockroaches, infestations, bureaucratic tangles, the constant traumas that put the families again in danger. We didn't know about the lack of jobs in Portland, nor did we fully understand the power of community, in populating an entire apartment building just with your own tribe, of creating a hedge in the midst of the storm. Perhaps we thought it a chance circumstance; I know that I personally found it miraculous—this little pocket, this small slice of rural, tribal life in the midst of the city. Since I had stumbled upon it so haphazardly, it felt like a gift to me. Life, which had consisted of either a bland, blank canvas or a series of anxiety-inducing decisions, had become crystallized. There would be places for me wherever I went, places that made me feel and think and see things differently. It did not have to be the square, beige box of the successful American story (already, even at age fifteen, the thought of years of academia and jobs seemed stifling and soul crushing). There was color to be found in all the gray.

Although there is much to deride, to pick at, to be disappointed about in typical evangelistic endeavors, I have much compassion for my younger self and her compatriots. We did not hesitate to teach our Bible stories or play games of soccer, to run around wildly, and to flail our arms just to see a child giggle. By the last day, the fifth day, we saw small signs of trust everywhere: the children running as fast as they could during the games, eating their snacks quickly and with great pleasure, proudly and stoically holding up their chunky, beaded bracelets for us to fall all over admiringly. We watched their little bodies slowly relaxing into this time, this vacation just a block away from life, and watched their faces get sleepy during the story time at the end, heads nodding in safety. And we loved them all, as best as we could love anyone outside of ourselves.

In the van, on the way back to our sheltered, comfortable lives, we talked about the successes. We congratulated ourselves on jobs well done, on the gospel being preached, on little children being saved. Sitting in the window seat, clutching my pillow, I didn't know what to think about all this language we were using; I could not put my finger on who or what had been evangelized, who had understood, who had been changed. But I could not get the images out of my head. The week would never leave me: the way the children all had sniffling colds, how they wore clothes that didn't quite fit. The glimpses I got into the kitchens, full of amazing smells, the walls covered in gorgeous, handwoven tapestries. The worn-out park we were in, with broken swings and dead, bristling grass, and the way it seemed that there was nobody there but us in the entire city.

They had preached to me, that entire week long. My small, compact world was starting to get bigger, my definitions of

Christian words growing and stretching. I had been blessed by these children I had been told were poor, sick, and sad. I didn't understand how clichéd it was, the way my experience had been turned upside down. Was this what evangelism was? Had we preached the kingdom of heaven? Was bringing the gospel always going to be so confusing?

I didn't know the answers yet, but I knew that I was being drawn to a life that might be more complex than I ever realized.

The Kingdom of Heaven

To follow my dream of becoming a missionary, of working full time with people who needed me, to chase that intoxicating feeling of discovering other worlds, I knew I needed training. So when I was nineteen, I enrolled in a Bible school in Portland. My mother, who is someone I can only describe as having an unquenchable thirst for God, raised me and my sisters on a steady diet of missionary biographies. The vast majority of them were about women: how they left all that they knew and any hope of a future to go and preach the good news. They were the original abolitionists, whistle-blowers, labor representatives, feminists. They went to be Jesus to the people that Jesus always went to: those that the powerful wanted nothing to do with. When I was young, I read about strong women, wearing tight buns and buttoned-up clothing, raising hell in India, China, Russia. I view it now as a rich legacy of service born out of racist and sexist theology: the mission field was one of the few places a woman could be in a place of leadership. And so the female preachers, teachers, and evangelists left the West, forsaking families and cultures that had no place for their gifts. And they brought liberation with them, wherever they went.

These missionary women were heroes to me, serving and liberating the lost and imprisoned, and they were all I had ever wanted to be. But once I was inside a classroom, getting down to the business of trying to convert others seemed to be a strange pursuit of study, attracting all sorts of even stranger people. The other students in my intercultural studies program were odd birds, every single one of them. Some were missionary kids themselves, all high-waisted jeans, polo shirts, and bad haircuts. Some of them were outsiders, people who could never make it in the landscape of the American church, which was increasingly putting a premium on pastors who could pack a place out, ministers who were in tune with the whims of pop culture. There were a few other earnest, big-hearted girls like myself, people who were passionate about studying Arabic and unreached people groups.

My school was small, conservative, grimly pleased with its own commitment to reading the Bible in a logical and sound way. The classes in our program were a throwback to another time, one in which people prepared for life lived in the jungle, for explaining the four spiritual laws, and where we watched videos on the demonic dangers of yoga. This instruction-from-another-era vibe wasn't helped by the orange plastic chairs and the worn-out brown carpeting; but I was charmed by it. In my dreams I saw myself as someone better suited for a simpler time: clutching my Bible to my chest, venturing out into the world, preparing to make disciples of all nations. These visions did not work anywhere but inside the classroom; the rest of the world only wanted to mock or chastise me for my visions of saving others.

Thus, in many ways my classes were a break from reality. I could finally engage who I really was, a girl who fantasized about preaching in the underground church in Belarus, a girl who wanted to live in an Indian orphanage, or an African hospital, or a Chinese school. Wherever there was danger, persecution, a lack of resources and education and gospel witness—this is where I wanted to go. I loved Jesus, of course, that was always in the back of my mind. But in reality, what I wanted more than anything was to be of use to somebody.

I distinctly remember one class where we read an entire book on the concept of the kingdom of God, and what it meant to "announce" it to the world. It became a running joke in the class: every day I would ask the professor, "So, just what exactly *is* the kingdom of God?" And every class he would answer, in long, drawn-out, theologically precise and difficult terms, using our textbook and various scriptures as his references. They were words I had heard my whole life, and they meant nothing to me. I was as blank as a piece of paper, and my poor professor knew it. He would always end his answer by trailing off, giving the definition that I could recite forward and backward. "The kingdom of God," he would say, his exasperation with me mingled with much love and care, "is wherever the rule and reign of God is found."

Satisfied with his answer, the professor would get back to teaching the rest of us about how we were supposed to go about telling people of this kingdom. But I couldn't do anything but sit in my uncomfortable plastic chair, my notebook empty and wide in front of me. The trouble was, most of the people I knew would say that God's rule and reign were in their lives. But what did that mean? We all said we loved God, we studied his Word with fervor, we cried when we sang songs, we saluted both the Christian and American flags in church. We celebrated his rule, we longed for his reign in our lives. And yet, we were still full of pettiness, greed, selfishness, pride, anger, lust—we still lived our lives entirely for ourselves, even in the missions department. I was only just starting to realize the disparities between what we say we want and what we actually desire.

I felt like I was looking and looking for this kingdom and had yet to find it; at the same time, I was supposed to be revealing it to others. What does a world look like where God is in charge? I assumed it looked like a world where we all got on our knees, repented, were saved, and then—what, exactly? But I didn't have those questions and words yet, just the lingering suspicion that a concept that so flooded the teachings of Jesus should mean more than rote allegiance to a blandly powerful deity. And since I did not know what it meant for myself, the implications of *announcing* this supposed new kingdom were anxiety producing, to say the least.

What was I going to Bible college for, immersing myself in stories so strange I could barely believe them? I was young, sheltered, with the smooth skin and self-assurance of the privileged, the one who doesn't quite understand what it means to be under a different kind of kingdom, the one in which the devil rules. I had only ever lived with Jesus, and so he didn't seem that important to me. I didn't need him, was the trouble.

Because the other, opposite kingdom, this country I call home—what I would now call the Empire—had been very, very good to me.

Back in the day, people thought Jesus had come as a political messiah. It was their fervent hope that he was there to overthrow the oppressive Roman government and usher in the glory of Israel once again. But to everyone's horror, Jesus proved them dead wrong, going on and on about the importance of women and children and foreigners and how there was no room for riches and the religious in his kingdom. He was there to throw open the gates, to tell God's chosen people that it was time to share their salvation, their money, and their time. It was all very subversive, very upside down.

But of course his platform, the number-one thing he talked

about, was the kingdom of God. For many years, Christians have read and absorbed "the kingdom of God" as a spiritual concept. It is, as my professor recited over and over to me, the rule and reign of Christ in the believer's heart. This is actually pretty convenient theology: believe in Jesus, go to heaven. However, reading Jesus's words it becomes apparent that the kingdom is very much about the here and now, changing the world to reflect what God desires: the oppressed would have justice, the poor would be fed, and the stateless wanderers would be taken care of. When taken literally, that "kingdom" Jesus was always talking about becomes very inconvenient indeed, primarily because we are supposed to be the ones bringing it.

Once this sinks in, you can't just live with your eyes to the sky anymore. At least, this was my experience. It becomes hard to sing about the love of Jesus while children starve to death halfway across the world. It becomes difficult to claim the blessings of God amid an economic system that benefits you but not your neighbor. And a country that claims to love the poor and huddled masses, but fiercely hoards her wealth and opportunities, starts to look increasingly sinful in the light of a longed-for kingdom where a loving God is in charge.

Early on I realized the people I most mirrored in the Bible were those blasted Pharisees, the ones who tried so hard their entire lives to be good, to work hard, to correct the thinking of others. They too were probably grimly proud of the way they memorized passages of scripture, how they could out-argue anyone, how they kept their society neat and clean of any moral gray. And so when I was in Bible college, when I read and read and read the words of Jesus, when I saw how his life was a continuous announcement of some mysterious amorphous thing called the kingdom of God, I became very scared indeed—because I didn't understand what the good news of the kingdom was, or how to bring it to earth, or how to be a Christian in a world that doesn't value taking care of others.

But instead of shutting my Bible and curling up in a corner to cry, I just kept on asking the question over and over again.

It is no accident that right around the time I first started hanging out with my Somali Bantu friends I started to get stuck like a scratched record on the question of what God was up to in our world. They were the ones, after all, who showed me the dual realities of life. Of how some have it hard, and how others do not.

Firmly on the latter side, once I began to get an inkling of how unjust things were for the majority of people in the world, I was lost. I looped constantly on these questions. Why is it so unfair? If God is love, then why does it feel so dark for so many? My questions were timid, shoved to the back of my mind, but they grew. At my Bible college, the answers poured forth like beautiful water, meant to satiate our minds. But all I saw was a crystal-clear stream, and I immediately wanted to thrash around in it, to muddy up those waters. I started to distrust the books, the men, the self-assured nature of the young and sound of mind. I needed the truth, but I needed it to come from a similar question-asker. I needed platitudes, but they needed to come from a bruised place.

There were certain professors who helped, men with shabby elbow patches and wicked intellects who gently talked to me about the now-and-not-yet of the kingdom. How it was here—how some people were miraculously healed, addictions broken, babies born, community forged—and how it was not fully here—death and disease and sin and sadness. The

Bible, too, started to transform in front of my eyes: it was so bloody, so messy, so full of trauma. The stories within were all sharp claws and edges, never as neat as I had been taught in Sunday school. Everyone was so horribly messed up, and yet God loved them, God used them, God was coming, he was bringing his kingdom, it was already here. And I started to believe, felt it growing inside of me, a real faith springing up through rocks.

Jesus once gave a sermon on the plain. He came down from a mountaintop to a level place where he could speak to his disciples and followers, to the devout or the curious. This sermon is carefully transcribed in the sixth chapter of the book of Luke, and it is markedly different from the more famous (and grander sounding) Sermon on the Mount. In Luke, Jesus upends everything we know about religion and success:

> *Blessed are you who are poor, for yours is the kingdom of God. Blessed are you who are hungry now, for you shall be satisfied. Blessed are you who weep now, for you shall laugh. Blessed are you when people hate you and when they exclude you and revile you and spurn your name as evil, on account of the Son of Man! Rejoice in that day, and leap for joy, for behold, your reward is great in heaven; for so their fathers did to the prophets.* (6:20–23 ESV)

This is not how the world works, I already knew that at the tender age of nineteen. But it meant a lot to know that the God I was following believed that this is how it should be. There was a different set of principles for the world of Christ, and I was slowly getting an inkling of how different they were from those of my country, my peers, and even my religious institutions. In this kingdom, the people I had been taught to save and redeem were the ones that were blessed, according to Jesus himself. This both shook me to the core and yet confirmed what I already knew: the life of strong-arming myself into a perfect representation of a loving God had done nothing for me. As I had seen from my own years growing up fully immersed in God's chosen people, I already knew that right thinking did not necessarily lead to right action, and Jesus seemed to be very concerned with both. And so I stopped asking the question, and set off to see it in action myself.

I consider this a pivotal point in my conversion story. I was never one of those kids with a good testimony, a story full of intoxicating addictions, the appeal of the sinner-turned-saved. I was destined for the far murkier sands of the religious upright, inadvertently becoming someone who was so good that they didn't need saving anymore. Instead, I was converted slowly, as I had my life ruined and fitfully tried to live like my savior, to place his values before my own. Jesus had been deeply involved in the lives of desperate people in his own life, and he cared about sickness and inequality and poverty and spiritual starvation. He ran toward the places I had been taught to move away from, the opposite direction from where I and all my classmates were headed. But as I learned to have new eyes, I began to see that he might have a place for me there, on the margins of society—that I could become a listener, and give up on my ideas of power and prestige and saving us all. This kingdom would be good news, in the long run, for us all.

This understanding propelled me out of the classroom and into the world. Without being able to articulate it, I too was desperate to experience the miracles of the kingdom. This entailed a certain amount of creating the room for that to happen, for pitching my tent with all the people that Jesus promised would be blessed. As I marched off on my own road, farther and farther away from the places that the Empire was telling me were only full of good things, I was not afraid.

As always, in retrospect, I probably should have been.

One day, not long after that Christmas party where I first felt the stirrings of where my life was headed, I followed a nice young lady from a local nonprofit organization to a battered apartment complex on the outer east side of Portland. The deeper you went into the complexes, the more the curtain of the Western world fell away: here, time stood still. Nobody had cars, nobody had jobs: everyone came with their culture weighing heavy on their backs and precious little more.

When I had signed up to volunteer with the refugees, I immediately noticed the harried and dazed looks of the sweet-souled people who worked for this charity organization. They were in over their heads. As it would turn out, the Somali Bantu were some of the least successfully acclimated refugees the United States ever attempted to resettle. When I met them, fresh out of a decade or so of awaiting their fates in refugee camps, many of them had never used a light switch or indoor plumbing, or even climbed stairs. I saw the shock of America through their eyes, and it was very sobering indeed. When I went into the nonprofit office to sign up to help, it was not yet clear how difficult it would be to force these resilient and stricken families to assimilate into a culture still besotted with manifest destiny. The cards stacked against them were typical of many immigrants: clashing cultures, an unfamiliarity with American concepts such as buying on credit (and paying it back plus crippling interest), language barriers, and social service applications.

The Somali Bantu are a people who have been kicked in the teeth by the world. The Bantu are descendants of ethnic tribes from Southeast Africa who were captured in the nineteenth-century Arab slave trade and sold in Somalia (and other parts of Northeast Africa and Asia). They are ethnically and culturally diverse from the majority Somali clans and have been subject to marginalization as a result of their slave status. I slowly, in fits and starts, learned how these people, my friends, had experienced multiple human rights violations in their recent past, how they had been denied access to education and other basic needs in their native country by the majority ethnic groups. I learned that when the violence broke out between the warring tribes and clans in Somalia, the Bantu were the first to feel shocks—much of their farming and agriculture was taken, or burned, unspeakable acts were done to the women and children, and so many men were killed.

It's amazing how much I didn't know, how to this day there is still so much left in the gray. But from the moment I met them, I knew at once that they were not immigrants hewing closely to the origin story we like to tell about ourselves and our country. These were individuals who had been forced by unbelievable trauma to leave everything behind. As Warsan Shire, the Somali poet writes: "no one leaves home unless home is the mouth of a shark / you only run for the border when you see the whole city running as well." The Somali Bantu refugees I met were polite, they were grateful, they were intent on surviving. But they were not happy to leave their country, fraught as it might have been. I wonder if right from the moment they stepped on the ground, they sensed it: the American Dream had no place for them. And yet, here they were.

The day my background check cleared, the nice volunteer-mobilizer lady called me and took me to meet the family I had been assigned to. Ostensibly I was going to be their English tutor, and I arrived armed with a few feeble papers. As my car crept slowly into its parking spot, I realized I had never felt more fraudulent. I was a young, covert missionary with a terrible grasp of English grammar. I knew I would be found out within seconds. And yet, I couldn't contain the feeling of excitement that this was where I was supposed to be. I had found my work, and therefore my place, in the kingdom.

The nice volunteer-mobilizer lady marched up to a door on the ground level and introduced me to the several adults scattered around on misshapen couches. She tried to explain that I was there to teach English and made it clear that my number-one-priority student was the mother of that particular family, Jamila.

I had been told that Jamila was a lot of fun, always laughing and bumping shoulders, eager to please. To me, she was terrifying. Older and wiser with an inscrutable past, when she did not smile at me I felt as small and as ignorant as a toddler. Luckily, she did smile at me most of the time, especially in the beginning.

Jamila dragged a couple of folding chairs into the weak January sun and we sat in a circle in the middle of the parking lot. This would be the first of many times I realized how silence can be comforting in its own way, how I could take a break from the pressures of American culture for a minute. The nice volunteer-mobilizer lady introduced me to the rest of Jamila's family, and I tried to keep up: there was Abdi, Jamila's husband—a grand, tall man with a dignified hat and cane who kept a respectful distance. Of all the children running around, two were Jamila's youngest daughters, Saida and Khadija, born eighteen months apart and around six and seven years old. Her oldest daughter Hali was inside, dutifully cooking the evening meal of pasta and boiled potatoes, adept at cooking even though she was barely ten. Her oldest son Mustaf was elsewhere, perhaps hanging out at a nearby apartment with his sweetheart Maryan, laughing, joking, and flirting in the teenage way that transcended all cultures.

The children openly stared, and we adults smiled politely. Much later, as I grew closer to Saida and Khadija, they giggled as they told me that everyone thought I was a boy for the first few weeks, because my hair was cut so short. As instructed, I went over a simple ESL worksheet or two with Jamila, encouraging her as she repeated the sounds of the alphabet with me. We waved goodbye and I was filled with both a sense of relief that it was over and a prickling longing to return as soon as possible. Later, back at the office, I signed a contract saying I would hang out with Jamila and her family no less than three hours a week for the foreseeable future.

By the third or fourth time I showed up, kicking up a crowd of children in my wake (terrifying me with their fascination with my moving car), I realized Jamila had no interest in learning English. She would humor me for a few minutes, and we would laugh and mime and talk about whatever she was cooking and I would try to get straight the names and ages of all the kids hanging around, trying to piece together who belonged to who (there were five Somali Bantu families at this particular complex). And then Jamila would get up from her chair and go off to finish cooking, the lesson closed with an air of finality that I could not argue with.

I eventually grew tired of sitting by myself in a metal folding chair, waiting for an eager tutee. There was only so much

I could talk about with the other women milling about, and the men were either nonexistent or smoking under the trees, looking at me suspiciously. After the novelty wore off, no one knew what to do with me—an unmarried girl with all her hair cut off.

I started to sit on the floor, where the children were, and I tried to help with their schoolwork. I tried to explain word problems to children that had never held a pencil in their life. It was ridiculous trying to quantify young Johnny's problems with counting apples in a barrel with children who still wondered if there was enough rice for everyone to eat the next meal. Around us people would be moving in and out of the apartment, speaking in a tone and at volumes that sounded harsh to my ears. The women would roll in like mountains, masses of flesh encased in beautiful, shimmery cloaks. They terrified me with their shouting and complete and utter mastery of the household.

I became a familiar piece of the scenery: the blurry white girl with the good intentions. The children, who were so accommodating to any hints of affection, were by far the easiest. More and more of my time was taken up by them: finding clothes for the winter, getting vaccinations for school, playing a defeatist game of trying to catch up to grade level. For the adults, I became a glorified errand girl (I had a car!). I didn't mind being used, because at least it meant I was useful.

I have a few pictures from this time, taken in a whirlwind of those first few months: the silhouettes of children, unsmiling, sitting on haphazard couches, watching TV; walls painted a low-income beige; official-looking envelopes lying on the counters, unopened and unread. A large tin plate of rice sits on the counter, a stew bubbles on the stove. Adults sit in the bare-looking rooms, fanning themselves, getting up the energy to brave the wilds of the nearest grocery store, two bus stops away. A cane is lying on a mattress in the middle of the room, a bag of spicy hot Cheetos and an empty bottle of Orange Fanta on a coffee table.

The families in my pictures are confused, disoriented, angry, hopeful, and very, very tired. Nobody in Jamila's family can read, and the English phrases they know can be counted on two hands. They are shocked to find they are still living in survival mode, although they no longer have to worry about lions, soldiers, or starvation. But there are different predators, all around, waiting for the first sign of weakness.

There are apartments like the ones I knew so well all over America, I've learned. The poor, crammed into apartment buildings and high-rises, dilapidated houses in neglected urban centers: huge concentrations of them placed where they can easily be avoided by those already on the upward mobility path. Managed by a bureaucracy with an ideology of containment, the poor are not so much helped by our government and our charities as they are hidden away. Keep them alive, keep them fed, keep some sort of a roof over their head. And keep them away from everyone else.

If I hadn't been driven there by the nice volunteer-mobilizer lady, I would never have known that beyond the asphalt and concrete jungles there were entire tribes of people struggling to make a life. There were people, like Jamila and her family, who had experienced more trauma, more displacement, and more tragedy than I could ever dream of. And they were starting to realize that perhaps America was not the land that was so promised to them. They had made the long and arduous journey over, and now the hard part had begun.

Because of my new friends, I experienced other worlds as

well: the hallways of social service organizations, the tangled phone lines of predatory lenders, the endless paperwork of the resettlement agencies. I experienced the ways that people looked at my friends out in public, how their eyes traveled up and down the head scarves, how they squinted their eyes, and how they wondered aloud if the Somalis were speaking Arabic. I was there when some of the girls came home from school, tears in their eyes, the first time someone told them to go back to their country. The cruelty of children, burning like fire. If only they knew how much that was wished for and how it would never be a reality. If only, if only, if only they could go back.

A year or two after meeting Jamila, I ask Mustaf, her oldest son, which one was better: Africa or America?

He pauses a moment, carefully considering his answer. He works long hours driving a medical transport car; he just got married and has a baby on the way.

In Africa, he says, you were always thinking about how you would get food. In the camps, this is all you need. But here, he says, and his voice trails off a bit. Here, everything costs so much money and you must work all the time to pay for everything.

He looks at me as he says it, like he is embarrassed for me, like he does not want to shame me.

Both places are the same, he says. Both places are very, very hard.

Hungry

When I was young, the communion we took at church seemed so delicate and rarified—tiny plastic cups of grape juice that crunched pleasantly underfoot, little uniform slivers of unleavened bread as tiny as a caterpillar. The day I professed that Jesus was Lord of my life and was baptized was the day I was officially allowed to participate in the ritual. I was six years old.

As I sat straight in my pew, sipping out of that tiny cup, swallowing the mere morsel of bread, I knew I was now a part of the community. I couldn't possibly know the rest of it—what broken flesh really looks like, how blood is warm and electrifying. I didn't know that death was real, and so my sense of resurrection was very, very small. And as I grew, I just didn't think of it that much. I participated in the ritual, took the tiny portions and washed the blood and body down without a second thought, week after week after week. It was a neat and tidy ritual that took five minutes to accomplish in an entire church full of people with their heads bowed, waiting for the worship leader to break into another song about love.

I got so used to the sight of those tiny little slivers, those plastic cups of juice, that they simply didn't mean anything much to me. Same as with the pictures and images I had of Jesus. I had known him my whole life and knew there was something of terrible importance there. I ate and drank of his body, but it did not move me.

As it turns out, the problem wasn't that I didn't understand the significance of communion. It was that I wasn't hungry to begin with.

In Bible college, I was learning how to evangelize, how to convert those who believed differently than I did. Meeting the refugees was like enrolling in a practicum course: I could use all the tips and tricks I was learning in the classroom and implement them in the real world. Except, of course, nothing ever happened like it did in the textbooks.

I took classes on how to make the gospel contextual to Muslims, where I listened to theories and strategies and took furious notes. And then I would rush out the door, to my very-Muslim refugee friends and try out all my new material. And I bombed, over and over and over again, failing to present the gospel in any relevant way to the Somali Bantu. I received blank looks, condescending pats on the knee, annoyed brush-offs, and more than a few intense confrontations. But each failure was just devastating enough that I would resolve to brush myself off, go read some more Bible, and try again the next day. It only made me more passionate, driven, and willing to try anything. Eventually, I learned to listen, which is without a doubt the most important missionary skill.

All of this started to matter less and less to me as time went on. It took a year or so, but I finally ran out of ways to practice converting my friends. After showing things like the Jesus film, dropping off Bibles in Arabic (which they couldn't read), and trying to bring up discussions of Muhammad and Jesus (which invariably led to blank looks and disquieted murmurings at my expense), I gave up. I sat back on their couches and chairs, and sank into the reality of the situation. *This is how it is,* I thought, *and there was no room for an agenda, even if I wanted one.* I was supposed to arrive full of answers and arguments; I was supposed to be filled to overflowing with the good and logical news of salvation. But I was only just starting to realize how very hungry and thirsty I was, how my new friends had stirred up in me questions that could not be rationalized away.

Over long, hard years I unlearned the lessons those books taught me, how to be right and do right, and to figure out the untamable One. But still, I am grateful for those years of Bible college, of trudging up rain-soaked sidewalks, sitting in dingy orange chairs under flickering fluorescent lights, doubting and questioning and ultimately believing in it all, albeit in new ways. Outside of the classroom, I learned again and again that there are stories to be listened to, a kingdom to be established, a life to be lived for the sake of others. And inside, I continued to get hungrier and hungrier.

I heard a story from a friend the other day, someone who spent many years living in Cambodia. He told me about entering a prison, a place of darkness and desperation, and of talking about Jesus there. The prisoners, all men, wanted to know more about Christ. The whole story was told—the healings and teachings he performed as he walked the earth, his death and resurrection, his promise that he was at the right hand of God the Father, preparing a place for them in eternity. The men professed interest and even belief; Jesus sounded good to them, and they wanted in.

My friend told me that they decided to have a communion service with the prisoners, and brought some juice in a cup and a baguette of fresh bread. My friend took the loaf and broke it in two, uttering the words that Jesus spoke at his last Passover meal: "This is my body, broken for you." He tore the bread in half and handed it to the prisoner on his right. He held up the cup of juice, and referenced Jesus again: "This is my blood, shed for you." As he started to pass the cup, he noticed something strange. My friend had grown up in America, where he was used to people breaking off tiny hunks of bread and then dipping it into the juice as it passed, each one repeating the refrain of Christ.

But here, in the Cambodian prison, the men were taking huge chunks of bread. So large, in fact, that after several prisoners had received communion there was no bread left. My friend, not unkindly, asked the first few men why they had taken such large pieces of the baguette when there were other people waiting to receive.

One of the men spoke up, voicing what they all had been feeling. They were hungry, of course, but that wasn't their reasoning. "You told us this bread was the actual body of Christ, and we want as much of him as we can get." The men around the room nodded, hungry and thirsty for all of it. Who could stand for a little piece of Jesus, when you could have a large portion? They were positively greedy for Jesus, needed him as only the hungry can.

At that moment, my friend knew that the prisoners were right. He went out and bought several more baguettes, and in the prison that day there was a feast. And my friend told me how it was the best, truest communion he had ever been a part of. He left that prison that day feeling filled for the first time in years, blessed to experience Jesus with the hungry.

It is a paradoxical place: one must first be hungry in order to be satisfied.

Cockroaches

Before I lived in low-income apartments, I understood that pests could be avoided. I assumed that they were tied to uncleanliness, a harbinger of slothful intentions, of squalor, completely avoidable if one made the right choices. But I soon found out that this is not the case, and it was very humbling. I have now lived in various low-income apartments for the better part of a decade, and battling bugs has become a part of my life. This most recent time, in an old and rather grungy apartment complex built in the seventies, the cockroaches got so bad that I developed a twitch any time I had to turn on the lights after it got dark. Watching the creatures scurry to the corners of our kitchen, I would shudder. Like many of my neighbors, I manically tried to clean and spray and contain any food or water source, but I was battling bugs who had evolved for this very purpose: to survive, to shame me, to win.

Married now, my husband and I talked to our landlord about it, and he got a professional exterminator to come out. In my memory, the exterminator is a young man in a dark gray jumpsuit, a big heavy bag of chemicals in hand. He leans on the doorframe and explains that the bugs will go away for a while, and then they will come back. Where do they go? They flee the poison and go to the next apartment over and the one after that. I am stricken by that thought. I shall be free of the pests for a few months, but my neighbors will experience the swarm. Here

I was, trying to live and love my neighbors as God loved me, but I was willing to inflict a pestilence on them just in order to have a bit of peace myself.

The man was right. The cockroaches went away for a while, and then they came back. So did the mice, which our cat was content to watch race over our floors while she napped with one eye open. So did the ants, which burrowed up through our carpet and created anthills in our living room. We were fighting a battle with decay that we never won, and the little creatures were always a signifier of this.

The one plus of all this was the knowledge that so many others were dealing with the same problems. We were all in this together, and it lessened the sting of it just a bit.

A few months after I met them, I discovered that Jamila and her family had to move. Her husband, Abdi, was very ill, and had been for some time. They were moving into low-income housing that had been built for people just like them, the ones hovering on the margins of society: refugees, the post-homeless, single moms, and others from situations of generational poverty. The new apartment complexes smelled of fresh white paint and possibilities; they were named after the first Native American saint, a somewhat-too-late testament to the history of how the majority often responds to the minority.

I found out about the move like I found out about most things having to do with Jamila and her family: I showed up one afternoon, prepared for English lessons, homework, or a recycling run and found mattresses piled in the damp parking lot. Other neighbors, all either Somali Bantu themselves or Turkish refugees (who all spoke Russian, in an odd turn of events), sat on their balconies and smoked as they watched the proceedings. There were no boxes and not a moving truck in sight. Through a series of conversations with anybody I could find, I eventually got passed a cell phone and chatted with a man named "the Sheik," who was famous to me even back then. The Sheik was a Somali man who seemed to run everything, acting as a liaison between the various charities that sponsored the refugees and communicating with the families themselves. He was the one you talked to when you had problems, who could help you out in a pinch. While he was seemingly good natured, I never had a good feeling about the Sheik, which was confirmed years later when through the grapevine I heard about the myriad of "wives" he had, his preferred choice of payment for services rendered. But on this day, moving day, I was glad to have an English speaker on the phone.

The Sheik promised me that he had a moving van lined up, but I was not convinced. I called a friend, and we decided to move old-school style—throwing pots, pans, and bedding willy-nilly into our battered sedans, using large black trash bags for everything else. We made several trips to the new place, where the children bounced excitedly from pristine room to pristine room, marveling at the luxury of three separate bedrooms. I picked up several pizzas and a few liters of coke, because that was what I had been trained to do in these situations. The children ate like they were famished while the adults politely sipped their soda.

After our last load, we got down to the business of cleaning the old place. The kitchen was coated with a thin layer of dust, the unfortunate combination of cooking oil and dust creating a Teflon-like layer of grime. The dishwasher had never been used for its intended purpose, instead being used to store clothes and dishes that weren't in use. The stove was a testament to nearly a year's worth of fried and bubbling food. Whenever I had been in the kitchen previously, the same battered pots and pans were being used in a constant combination of cooking, serving, and cooking some more. I instructed several of Jamila's friends to wipe down the cabinets in the kitchen, and they did so with somewhat quizzical expressions (trying to explain the concept of a security deposit was useless, and back then I didn't know that the landlords in charge of these types of deposits would never return the money regardless). I set to work cleaning the large sliding glass doors that led to the parking lot, starting with the long vertical blinds that served as a bit of privacy into the living room. As I went up and down the blinds, catching the same oil/dust mixture on my bit of rag, a shower of something that felt like tiny pebbles rained down on my head and shoulders. Confused, I shook my hair and started to brush off my shoulders. It took several seconds for me to realize the dirt that had just fallen on me was *moving,* hundreds of tiny (and not-so-tiny) cockroaches wiggling about. I looked up, and to my horror discovered nests up in the folds of the blinds. I shrieked, dancing around as I swatted at my head and shoulders, over and over again. A few of the kids saw what happened and laughed, pointing and collapsing on the floor.

I got it together just in time. Closing my eyes and willing myself not to freak out, I stood still and quiet for a moment or two. Then I grabbed a broom and whacked the blinds until no more cockroaches fell out, after which I sprayed chemicals maniacally, my eyes steely. I sprayed until the creatures stopped squirming, until the floor was wet with damp little bodies and the chemicals made us cough, throats burning. I declared that we were taking a break, and we all went outside to sit in the grass, watching the children kick a half-inflated ball around the parking lot.

The kids were still making fun of me; I could see them re-enacting my cockroach dance, complete with small shrieks. The adults seemed to catch on too, as several of them came over and clasped my upper arm, pointing to the blinds and laughing. I felt tired, filthy, and spooked by the feeling of tiny legs running along my neck. But as I sat in the grass, exhausted by all the elements of moving a large family, even if they had only a small percentage of the belongings of a typical American family, I smiled into the gray, cloudy late afternoon.

It was kind of funny, after all. I allowed myself to enjoy being made fun of, to view it as a blessing of inclusion on that fine fall afternoon. I laid down in the grass and closed my eyes, once again confused by how something so new and different could feel so much like home.

Back then, I was naive and enthusiastic and excited about the life that was ahead of me. It would not always be this way, and I'd experience deep lows that would shock my younger, self-assured self. But even now, a full decade later, as I clean and scour and search for signs of bugs in yet another low-income apartment, listening to the sounds of my neighbors cooking and cleaning and laughing and yelling at their children, I am astonished that this is where I live. That I get to experience the complexity of living in relationship with people at the margins of society, people who have to be resilient in so many ways. That I get to experience so much of the hospitality, the community, the blessings of living cheek-to-cheek with refugees and those who grew up in generational poverty is not lost on me.

The kingdom of God is like a pearl, a mustard seed, a lost coin that you will turn your entire life upside down to find. I had heard all of these metaphors, and more, since the time I was a small child. When I went off into the world to find these seemingly small and insignificant signs of a very good God at work in the world, I was surprised by what I found. The kingdom of God was so small, like a nest of cockroaches, a workbook full of scribbles and scratches, shared laughter over the absurdities of the world. It was everywhere I looked; in the end, I just needed the eyes to see it.

2

Reality Sets In

Language Learning

In the beginning, it felt like I was living out my dream, digging into the good, hard work of the Lord. But slowly, the challenges started to pile up, and the reality of both the situation that my refugee friends found themselves in and the limits of my own cheerful goodwill started to weigh on me. As the easy answers and theologies never seemed to work, I was forced to contemplate what it meant to build tenuous webs of relationships with people who were radically different from me. As I started to put my theoretical missionary dreams into practice, I began to long for the days when it seemed that I actually had solutions to problems.

Learning the language of the group you are trying to reach is Missionary 101. I jumped into the process with vigor, not bothering to consider how little propensity I had shown for learning new languages in both high school and college. I just showed up and expected to learn by osmosis. As you can imagine, it was very slow going. The language of the Somali Bantu, *Maay Maay,* was just being written for the first time. There were rumors that the first Somali Bantu man to get his college degree was doing a dissertation on the language, right in my own city, but I could never reach him. There were no books, tapes, CDs, or classes that could help me in this endeavor. If I ever wanted to talk about God, then I had to learn Maay Maay. And so I tried to learn the way my friends had—by picking it up as I went: by sitting on the couch and praying that the words flowing around me would somehow sink in.

I would repeat the words I was hearing, and the older children, the teenagers, would look at me and shake their heads. No, no, I wasn't saying it right. The adults would just laugh or look without comprehension whenever I tried out my new words. Either my pronunciation really was that terrible (and I suspect it was), or they had no room to consider someone as different as me speaking their small, secret language. The children would shriek at me "No! No!" and then say the word I was trying to say again, louder and louder until they were practically screaming at me. Finally, they would give up, disgusted at how my mouth turned the words mealy. I felt helpless and defensive—I had no idea what I was doing wrong and had no way to fix it.

I begged them to write the words down on a piece of paper for me. They couldn't, which is when I first realized how far I had to go. And it turns out that I do not learn best by words being shouted at me, louder and louder with no explanation. So, my Maay Maay stayed in its miserable infancy state, never to grow and become real.

For months I still tried to be the good little volunteer, to show up on time and go over worksheets and leave after exactly three hours had passed. I would show Jamila a picture of the sun, and we would practice saying "Sunny. Sunny. It is sunny." And the next time I came around again, the same sheet of paper clutched in my hand, her eyes would hold no recognition for the words. It was like she was a blank canvas, smoothed every night by the troubles of getting by, of keeping the electricity on, of staying warm in the chill air, of finding any sort of food that looked familiar to cook. She had no space for the badly designed worksheets, my terrible drawings of weather conditions. I was young, I was impatient, and I really wanted to tell my new friends about the gospel. But I could see in Jamila's eyes that she was refusing to accept my language. Now I know that trauma robbed Jamila of memory retention and the ability to process new information.

Years later, I went back to school to get a degree in teaching English to speakers of other languages. Jamila and her friends and family were the direct inspiration for this change in studies, as my life slowly moved away from the spiritually abstract to a desire to meet the concrete and material needs I saw all around me. I learned how people from pre- or nonliterate communities are a unique minority in this day and age and how the challenges they face in navigating literacy-centric societies can be overwhelming. These communities tend to be rich in oral histories and strong familial and societal ties, but are at a disadvantage when it comes to deciphering abstract representations of objects, for instance. All those years ago, when I was showing Jamila a worksheet with a picture of a happy, smiling sun, to her it appeared as meaningless as a Q drawn with too many squiggles surrounding it. She did not tie those lines drawn on the paper to the great shining orb in the sky because she had not been raised to think that way. I did not know this, of course, and it was yet another exercise in trying to do good and failing miserably. It was another exercise in my refugee friends risking their own identities—being put in a position of showing their ignorance, of confessing to not understanding—just to welcome me into their homes to sit on their couches another day. To extend a relationship, when they did not have to.

I eventually managed to learn just enough of the language to get by with the kids. There was a period of time when I organized so many kid-related events I felt like a grubby, disheveled Mary-freaking-Poppins. The kids had nothing to do when school was off, and they followed me around hoping for a bit of fun or to try to bum some candy off me. I learned to say all the important words: "Hey, you! Stop it! Come here! Quickly, quickly. No, no, NO!!!!!" I also learned the somewhat complex

49

family dynamics of many of the kids (which took some time, trying to untangle who was an auntie, a mom, a sister, a cousin, or a general all-purpose relative), and I studied and memorized all the names of the mothers. As scared as I was by these strong, determined women, it was nothing to how the children felt. When a child misbehaved on my watch, I would pull them aside and whisper that I would tell their mama, that I knew which apartment she lived in, and I wasn't afraid to march up there and knock on the door. This, knowing the name of each child's mother, proved by far to be the most satisfactory disciplinary tactic. We were all afraid of the mamas.

I fell into similar rhythms with everyone else: the mothers and I would talk about how we were, what was cooking, how the family was, if they wanted to do English lessons. The fathers, always on the periphery, never paid me much mind until suddenly one of them would sit me down for a full-on lecture delivered in a rapid-fire manner in a language incomprehensible to me. If the adults really wanted to communicate with me, they fetched the older children, those on the brink of the teen years, the ones who were not only absorbing the language but also starting to realize all the vast cultural differences there were in this country as well: "Can you take us to the store, read our mail, call DHS, apply for energy assistance?" Those children, those stoic little adults, those translators of a life; I loved them so much that before they even finished asking me, I would say, "Yes, yes, let me help you in whatever way I can."

There is only so much rejection the heart can take, so I slowly stopped bringing my worksheets with me when I went to visit. Jamila already knew that she would never learn English; at the time, I couldn't see how she had devoted her energies into surviving, as she always had done. Once I accepted it and stopped showing up to teach, when I gave up my illusions of control, of mutual dialogue and understanding, and of my ability to witness with my words, life became significantly easier. I stopped trying to force the kingdom, stopped shining a blaring light on all of our deficits, on all that we didn't know or couldn't do—and that is when we actually started to resemble something like friends, something like neighbors.

I realized this some months later, when I walked into Jamila's apartment, my hands empty and prepared to do whatever it was they needed that day. I was surprised to find the place calm, the kids late at school, the apartment hushed and dimmed. Jamila was there, sitting on her old couch, watching something on the television. She looked up at me and smiled, and she motioned for me to come sit down next to her. I did, relishing the chance to be so close to this fierce, capable woman. I looked at the TV and was shocked to see a "Sweatin' to the Oldies" VHS tape playing, Richard Simmons in all of his spandex glory bouncing around while people in various stages of overweight tried to copy his hyperactive dance moves. Any time the camera would cut to a shot of the sweaty participants moving their arms and legs around, Jamila would start to giggle. Her laughter got louder and louder until she was shaking, trying to contain it and failing miserably. I sat next to her on the couch, and I saw just a tiny taste of America through her eyes—the loud music, the tight clothes, and the smiling, overweight participants—and it was ridiculous. I started to giggle too, and there we were—such different women, coming from such different cultures—both of us understanding how fragile the world is, how little grasp of anything we had. Why not laugh at what we found ridiculous, sitting stationary on a couch as we watched others huff and puff their way to glory, to accepting themselves as big and beautiful and worthy of encouragement and praise and neon shorts?

We lost ourselves in the moment, until we were wiping the tears from our eyes at the hilarity of the excesses and obsessions of American culture. And I think it was that moment where, slow and small like a seed, my fear of Jamila started to change into admiration. Perhaps we didn't need language to communicate after all.

Conversion

I love the living rooms of my refugee friends. I love seeing how they change over time, seeing how my friends both do and don't assimilate into American culture. I love the Christmas lights and yarn creations, the calendars from grocery stores, the faux Persian ornate curtains tacked to the walls. When I was living and working closely with the Somali Bantu, most of the families had very similar couches—long, boxy, stiff, and covered in jewel-toned velvet. They had become a signifier, the closest cultural equivalent to a bride price. The couches were imported, and I was told they cost thousands of dollars. When Jamila's oldest daughter got married, she received one as a present from the man who would be her son-in-law.

Not long ago, I sat on this couch, and I missed the girl for whom it was given. Jamila was next to me, watching two TVs side by side. Instead of Richard Simmons, on this day there was a video of a Somali wedding on one screen, from Texas I think, people slowly shuffling and dancing around a rec center. The music was blaring out of the television speakers, filling up the room. On the other screen was PBS Kids, some sort of cartoon about math or phonics. I had come over for homework help a bit early, and Jamila's children were not yet home. Since there were no children in the room, I wondered why the cartoon was on at all. For company, perhaps?

And then Jamila's youngest kids, Saida and Khadija, were

suddenly home from school, banging doors and throwing their heavy bags on the floor. As they fixed themselves a snack (peanut butter spread on old hamburger buns—the only food they had that day), they released an entire day's worth of pent-up information, the words spilling out of their mouths. They told me they wanted iPads, that they don't understand why Gotye is so popular ("in the music video, they just stand around and *are painted*"), that they saw *The Hunger Games* ("What was it about?" I asked. "I dunno. I think it was like the Olympics or something"). They settled in next to me on the couch, switched one of the TVs to the Disney Channel, and we watched it for a while.

I thought of the statistic that mentioned how the average American is exposed to over 3,000 advertisements in a single day, and it suddenly seemed like a very conservative estimate.

Later, in bed that night, I lay awake wondering: *Why aren't my Somali Bantu friends trying to convert me?* I was stuttering and stammering my way through talking about Jesus, using every opportunity of a headache or cold to offer to pray, both confident and afraid that God was going to come down and do something. And yet, my friends seemed content to practice their religion with no thought of asking me to join. It was a lonely thought—maybe I was not worth saving.

I used to think the goal of my life was to convert others. I didn't feel too badly about it, either. I was so sure that I had what these folks needed, that I had been graced with all of the right answers. The more I hung around on the periphery, the more my mission field started to unfold into complex backgrounds and the more all of history started to seem like a never-ending cycle of conversion. My Somali Bantu friends, like my own pagan ancestors, had been some variation of animists for centuries. They were forcibly converted to Islam sometime in the last century or so, the patterns of organized religion slowly changing culture and habits and beliefs. For me, with my little Western mind, it seemed clear: as literacy and education grow in the Somali Bantu community here in America, should they not be educated about other views regarding the greatest questions of our age? I, too, was greatly impacted by ideas of eternal damnation and a longing for everyone around me to be saved. And since it seemed to me that I was the only Christian hanging around the Somali Bantu community, that heavy yoke became mine alone to bear.

But the more I hung around and had my eyes opened to the realities of other religions and to my own, I slowly began to discover the real reason I was comfortable with my missionary dreams of convincing others of the truth: because it was becoming increasingly clear that we are all being converted, all the time.

On our first date, my future husband and I sat on a couch and watched a movie together. It turned out to be a movie about Africa, corruption, injustice, and the modern pharmaceutical companies making money off the poor. I tried to play it cool but ended up hysterical, sobbing so hard that I was gasping. I sat on the edge of the couch, my back straight as a rod, muttering, "I have to do something. I have to do something." The adorable bearded boy next to me awkwardly patted my back and tried to make me feel better, but it was too late. The date was over in my eyes. I would spend the next several hours turning the facts of inequality over in my mind, aware of how tied up my material comforts were to the suffering of the poor the world over. This happened to me from time to time. The veil of my supremely comfortable world would be ripped away from me, and I would be plunged into the realities of suffering from which I could not let myself escape.

That poor boy went home and told his roommate he didn't think the relationship was going to work out. "That girl," he told his roommate, shaking his head. "That girl is just a little too intense for me."

We got married in a fever. The theme of our wedding was 1970s missionary potluck reception (I searched everywhere for a church with orange pews, and we decorated with globes). We were young and materially poor and we were in love. We were going to school full time, working minimum-wage jobs. We were the caretakers at a megachurch, and we lived in an old, tiny farmhouse on the edge of the campus, rent-free. We got a cat. We started a band and played music in the upstairs attic. Sometimes we ate candy for dinner, just because we could. We lived in the suspended time of young love, and it was wonderful.

One night, squeezed together in the oversize armchair that served as our couch, we watched a documentary called *Another World Is Possible*. The film, full of shaky transitions and outdated hairdos, was about some of the evils in our world: wealth inequality, sweatshops, food industries—and what the Christian response should be. Again, a fire of belief was lit beneath me. It was all information I had heard before, but until this moment it had never mattered to me. There was some statistic, the numbers blurry in my brain, about the bazillions of dollars that Nike spends on mere seconds of advertising in Times Square. In contrast, it pays its underage and overworked employees in majority-world countries pennies an hour to make the very shoes on our feet. I watched children making the tennis shoes in question, in grainy, slow-motion footage, and I knew: I was connected to them by money and power and choice. My privilege and their suffering were closely linked, even as we all tried hard to forget.

By the end of the film I was crying, again: *I've got to do something. I've just got to do something.* This time my husband, too, was moved. Pale and quiet, we talked for hours about our role in a consumeristic, nationalistic culture. Our world suddenly changed again. *Another World Is Possible! Let's bring it about ourselves!* We became zealots of a kind, excited by the tangibility of our work. We could vote for a better world, every day, just by what we bought. We could change our patterns, no longer conform to a world that wanted us satiated but never satisfied. We vowed to buy only secondhand clothes. We started researching pacifism. We bought a Community Supported Agriculture box containing vegetables supplied by our refugee neighbors.

I loved how hard it was at first. It was proof that we were doing the good work. Every purchase was agonizing. We checked our labels, we researched all the companies, and we scrutinized our hobbies, free time, and media consumption. We would not exploit children with our cheap goods. We would not ruin countries with our excess and consumption. We would not lump entire groups of people in the category of "enemy" because they interfered with our political ideologies. For months we immersed ourselves in a crash course on learning about the systems of our American society and how they are built on oppressions of so many kinds. It was the beginning of believing that the kingdom that Jesus talked about was very much concerned with how we lived our lives, and that included how we spent our money and what kind of work we did.

Like all good new converts, we tried to get people to join our side. My sister would tell me about the cute jeans she just bought, and I would list off all the worker's compensation cases that exact company had, detailing the human rights abuses. We could pontificate on the importance of supporting local, seasonal agriculture. We wore secondhand clothes before they were cool. We opted out, loudly, of consumerism. And inside, we were pleased. We thought since we were undoing so many culturally conditioned habits, the hard part must be over.

During this time, I still drove my car thirty minutes downtown to hang out with my refugee friends several times a week. I found such a combination of pleasure and purpose and confusion in my relationships with the Somali Bantu refugees. I both dreaded and looked forward to my times in Little Somalia, as I was wont to call the apartment complex where seventeen families had moved.

I hung around long enough that when they built another low-income apartment complex across the street from Little Somalia, the managers asked my husband and me to move in. We looked at each other. I thought about living in solidarity with the poor, of being a radical obsessed with downward mobility. I thought, *Moving into low-income housing will be fun!* We will become the heroes and best friends of everyone in the complex. Our door will constantly revolve with streams of children looking for a warm environment for homework help, refugees learning English while laughing and drinking tea, people popping in to borrow sugar or drop off cookies. Everyone will love us. It was all so beautiful, in my mind. *Another World Is Possible.* We will make it so ourselves.

But, as it would turn out, moving in somewhere doesn't make you a neighbor. The idealism underpinning our desire to live in solidarity with the poor would end up taking so much time and energy that at night we found ourselves unable to do anything else but lock our doors and collapse in front of the TV. We moved in and discovered our neighbors were not simply good-hearted people who had been dealt a bad hand. Instead, they were complicated: they were exhausted single mothers who screamed at their children and smoked at the playground; they were the addicts, shut-ins, and the mentally ill; they were refugees who used us up and then asked us for more.

We were slowly shocked by the cost of human relationships. We didn't yet understand what it means to stick around long enough to experience the fullness of how messy life is on the margins. How much it hurts to teach little second-grade boys to read, and then watch them grow up and pretend that they don't know you in the elevator, laughing and joking with their friends, dressed head-to-toe in gang colors. Or to see the refugee girls I poured my life into let their dreams float away, never finishing high school and instead getting married at younger and younger ages, breaking my heart with each wedding. Or to be friends with the sick and watch them die, to witness relapses and abuses, to stand around and suffer with people you love. We didn't know the cost, and in a way I am so grateful.

Like all new converts, in the beginning we had it all figured out: stop buying new shoes. Move into the neighborhood. Eat kale until you want to die. Start an after-school program. Plant a community garden. Annoy all of your friends with your constant pleas to come help out. Start a community library. Never stop trying because you have got to do something, anything, to make the world a better place, a more equitable kingdom. We would gain a better world, even if it meant we might lose our souls.

If you had asked me in the midst of all of those years of learning and unlearning if it was worth it, I would have told you, yes. I would have looked you in the eye and told you the truth as straight as I could see it: *It is hard, but I am trying to convert to this way of living all the time; I expect I will be to the end of my days. And please forgive me, but I am trying to convert you along with me.*

On Pakora (and Mutuality)

Besides my friends from Somalia, there were other refugees who lived in the apartment complexes that my husband and I moved into. I once had a neighbor named Indu. She would crochet in her spare time when she was not busy watching her two-year-old son, a monstrously big child, both doughy and strong, who towered over my own toddler. Most of the surfaces in her apartment were covered in one type of yarned creation or another: the tables, the flat-screen TV, the kitchen chairs, the backs of the couches. In the doorways, into both the apartment itself and the two bedrooms down the hall, little balls of yarn hung, crocheted in alternating yellows and oranges to recreate marigolds from her home country, Bhutan. Her work was a welcoming, bright sight in this gray city. She chose colors randomly, it would seem, preferring brighter hues: electric blue, shocking pink, glowing orange. I loved how the colors made a bland apartment into something exploding with string carefully worked into patterns.

Indu lived just down the hall from me. We met in an English class in the community center across the street. I was drawn to her beauty, her smile, the way she communicated her answers with surety, proud of the work she had done. Quickly, our relationship shifted from one of teacher/student to one of equality. We both loved our children. We both became very tired of our children. We both liked to cook, to laugh, to get lost in reveries when looking out the window at the rain coming down yet again. We both needed friends.

She started to cook for me. I ate on tin plates, sitting on her crazy colorful chair covers. I ate white basmati rice, cooked to perfection. Dal, the standard lentil soup, was always off to the side in a small bowl, waiting to be poured over the rice. Sometimes there were dark-green vegetables, simmered with spices and chickpeas. Sometimes there was chicken, skin and bone still present, chopped to pieces, fried, and stewed. Usually there was a salad of red onion, yogurt, and cucumber. There were many other dishes, ones I never knew the names for but ate with relish, savoring every bite. I took spoonfuls of the red spicy pickle, as Indu watched in apprehension, and smeared it on my food. I ate with my hands, and the heat made my face turn red and warm. We would both laugh at the white girl who couldn't take the heat but craved it anyway. Indu would watch, hovering, never sitting with me, instead choosing to watch me. There was no need to put on a show; I loved every bite, and she was pleased to see it.

She loved to feed my child, so much smaller and blonder than her own. Without much coaxing, my toddler would gulp down the dal and shovel the rice into her mouth. Her eyes would get wide at the spice, and she would cough dramatically. And then her fingers would plunge in again, and she would eat until her belly poked through her shirt, Indu smiling small and proud the entire time. She told me that she wanted to cook lunch for my daughter every day; I politely told her I fed her myself sometimes, at our own apartment. As we watched my child eat like she was starving, we both knew that Indu did not fully believe me.

There came a day when I had to tell Indu that we were moving away from our apartments and English classes and meals. I watched as her face fell, seeing how it mirrored my own. We made plans for the next week; she was going to take my couch and my table, and I was going to eat her food one last time.

The time came. Her apartment looked spotless, my orange couch nestling into the corner. Her son played with the toys we didn't have room to bring with us, happy to slam plastic into plastic, my daughter content to watch. Indu was going to cook me my favorite dish, although I had never told her as much: pakora, deep-fried vegetables. This time, as a going-away present, she wanted to teach me how to make it myself.

I watched as she took a small green cabbage and a few red onions and sliced them thin. She mixed together chickpea flour, taking care to show me the bag (although it wasn't in English), milk, a generous helping of salt. She put in spices, but she didn't know their English names and bought them in bulk at the Indian grocery store. I watched, hoping to memorize the colors and the smells and the measurements, but they all look like some variation on summer yellow, and they all smell like the times I have sat at this table and eaten her food.

She mixed it all together in a metal bowl, slowly stirring with her hand in sweeping clockwise motions. I asked her how she knew when the oil on the stove is hot enough but not too hot and she just shrugged. She doesn't have the words. There are some things that she just can't tell me. It must come from cooking the foods you watched your own mother make, from countless shared experiences. I am used to recipes from magazines, trying exotic-sounding dishes once and then moving on. This does not make sense to my friend; she wonders why anyone would choose to not eat the food that has sustained her family for decades, the very best food in the world. After eating at her table for many months, I was starting to agree.

Indu dropped small lumps of the battered vegetables into the oil, crowding each other in the pot. A quick flip and they were done, transported to a basket lined with newspaper. They were meant to be eaten hot in the kitchen. She ate with me, that one and only time, both of us standing there watching the second batch cook. We were quiet and listened to our children in the other room, eating spicy hot Cheetos and marveling at the red powder that clung to their hands.

We lingered in the kitchen, and Indu made us chai in a small saucepan. The day was sunny and the apartment was a sleepy warm place near the end of summer. My daughter started to get clingy, pulling at my knees. I knew I had to leave, but I was slow to move toward the door. When I did, Indu shook her head side to side, still smiling. She wrapped up the leftovers from our feast and gave them to me for my husband. Serious now, she told me to cook for him and to cook for my baby. I felt nervous, all of a sudden. I watched her, so carefully, the entire afternoon, but I doubted my ability to reproduce anything this woman did. She had an entire history in her cooking habits, and it all came from someplace deep within.

In the beginning, when our friendship was still small and we were counting the steps, making mental notes of backgrounds and hierarchies, education and life experiences, I realized how much in her debt I was, and I didn't like it. Every meal she made, no matter how sharp and warm it tasted, was a meal that I would need to repay. As the months rolled on, this surfeit started to weigh on me, causing me anxiety.

I tried, in my own sorry way, to repay the favors. I tried cooking my kind of food for her: spaghetti (with turkey meatballs, the sacred cow being spared), pizza, Chinese stir-fry, a full Thanksgiving dinner. She never ate much, nor did she pretend to enjoy my food. When pressed, over and over again, she would say she simply wasn't hungry. On more than one occasion, she told me straight to my face that she didn't care for my food. Her forthrightness galled me, as I scraped unwanted food into containers. But after a few months of this, I decided to believe her. I slowly began to see how, to Indu, food is tied to her land and her people. Her extremely polite refusals of my food revealed her stubborn insistence on cooking and eating only what she knows. It is one small thing that she has control over in a life lived at the mercy of unjust circumstances. I only know her history from the bits she has told me, full of running from the police, making a life in a refugee camp, having babies in a place with limited access to food or medical care. And I have been privileged to see how Indu continually makes a life for herself, arranging any situation she has been given into a pattern that makes sense, one full of color and taste and home.

I never cooked for Indu again.

Our friendship blossomed because of this decision. Once I stepped back, when I embraced the inequality of the situation and allowed myself to be served, our relationship deepened. Those afternoons in her house became my reprieve, a time of true relaxation and commiseration in a very busy time of life. I was able, for the first time, to put myself in the position of the learner, the novice, the hungry. And the fruit of this living into these reversed roles was a truer friendship, the kind that changes people because it is based in real mutuality instead of a superficial desire for diversity.

Once I stopped cooking and started showing up with a healthy appetite, everything changed for Indu and me. The boundaries I put up between us dropped. I ate her food until I was full, my guilt relieved. There was no way I could repay her; the debt of hospitality was too high. But it was her pleasure to feed me, my daughter, and my husband to convey just the tiniest sliver of who she was and where she came from, and it was my pleasure to receive.

I once heard about a nun in the south side of Chicago who was the principal of the local Catholic school. In the 1970s, this particular school had experienced the changes in the neighborhood as more African-American families started moving in and "white flight" happened as a result. Eventually, the population at this Catholic school was almost entirely made up of black students. One day this nun went from classroom to classroom, and she changed the crucifixes hanging on the walls. In front of the students, this nun stood on a chair and took down the white-Jesus-dying-on-the-cross and replaced it with a black-Jesus-dying-on-the-cross. The students couldn't bear it. They had to ask their questions: "Sister, why are you doing that? Why are you changing the crucifixes?" Her answer was simple. "Well. We don't know exactly what Jesus looked like, but I am sure he looked more like you than he looked like me." I heard that story, and it caught my breath. I think about the kids in that classroom and what it meant to look up at a Jesus that looked like them. Because they were children, it must have burrowed deep into their spirits. Jesus was black, or at least not white in the way we define "white" in the United States. Jesus was an outsider. Jesus knew what it meant to never be at home in your own place.

I was born and raised in the church. In our conservative Christian setting, when I was a kid my life revolved around church services and Bible studies, and everyone I knew was just like me. I was in yet not of the world.

One of my favorite "Christianized" holidays growing up was Halloween. No one I knew celebrated what we considered to be "the devil's day." Instead, we all participated in something called a "harvest party." We would dress up in costumes, go to our churches, play a bunch of cheaply constructed games, and be rewarded with candy.

I was reminded about these alternative holidays after I had been working with Jamila and her family for several years. My husband and I had recently settled on attending a church after much deliberation (this one was too liberal, this one was too boring, this one was too sad, this one had too many ironic mustaches). We liked this particular church because people sang like they meant it, they clapped off beat, and the preacher shouted sometimes. Also, there was a picture of Black Jesus on the wall, which I thought was cool and edgy and reminded me of the nun in that Catholic school in Chicago.

It was this Black Jesus, with his kind eyes and dreadlocks, that gave me the false sense of security that we all would be welcomed at the upcoming harvest party, even the Somali Bantu girls whom I had asked to join. We had heard it said from the pulpit several times that this event was for the community. We were the community! And I felt sure we would be extra-liked, for we would be bringing the diversity. Everyone would feel self-congratulatory.

I had to talk my refugee friends into going. A few years earlier I had taken a van full of Somali Bantu kids to a harvest party at church next to my Bible college, where they ran around wild and stole candy from helpless little Spidermen. When I took the kids back to their apartment complex, the parents were incredibly upset with me. An older boy tried to translate, something about the belief that they would be cursed, as Muslims, for stepping foot inside a Christian church. In all of my hubris and arrogance, I waved away what I considered to be superstition. To myself I thought: *What nonsense. I'm studying Islam in school and I have never even heard of that belief.* But I could see that the parents meant business—that this was a big deal to them—and I had the sense to feel the tiniest bit of shame bloom up within.

But this year I had a bit more of a relationship to draw from, so even though I was nervous, I asked Jamila if her girls could come to church with me. The previous winter the girls had been flower girls in my wedding, and I had been overcome with the gift of the cultural risk they had taken in order to walk down the aisle of a church. They did it for me, and I did not take it lightly. So as Halloween rolled around I stressed the amount of free candy we would be receiving at the upcoming harvest party, and I was surprised that, with very little conversation, Jamila waved her hand in the air and surrendered. They could go. I asked them what they wanted to dress up as, and all three said, without skipping a beat: *princesses!* I tried to be cool about it, but this was rather disheartening. "Why do you want to be princesses so badly?" I asked, cagily. "We love Cinderella and Snow White so much," they sighed. "They are so, so, so beautiful!"

I made some pointed remarks about how I thought Jasmine and Mulan were pretty cool, only to be met with scorn. Finally, I rummaged around in my closet and found a bunch of Punjabi suits from my missionary stint in India at age seventeen and shouted: "Bollywood princesses!" I was so proud of the compromise I had come up with. I whipped up a couple of crowns with cardboard and copious amounts of glitter, put a bunch of gold eyeshadow on them, and dressed them up to look like glamorous Indian movie stars (we did keep the head scarves on, naturally). They *loved* it. They begged me to take pictures and hammed it up for the camera, as unselfconscious as I had ever seen them. My husband, due to his overgrown beard and penchant for flannel, took up a toy ax and instantly became a lumberjack. I went as myself: the embarrassingly earnest volunteer.

And then we got there, and we were definitely the uncool kids at the junior high dance. Everyone stared at us. You would think they had never seen a young couple in their twenties hanging out with a bunch of strangely dressed African Muslim girls before. Also, we seemed to have missed the memo that the party was geared toward toddlers. My girls stood around, towering over all the little white kids running around, becoming increasingly aware that everyone was staring at them. The girls tried to navigate the strangely complex system of traveling to different stations to play different cheap games in exchange for stickers, which they could turn in for a bag of candy once all the stations were done. Nobody talked to us. Nobody welcomed us. We were alone in a sea of people who all looked alike and who all seemed to know each other.

The girls are smart, and they knew they didn't fit in. And as they recognized their Otherness through the views of these church people, they shrunk into themselves a little bit more. I could see the change, see it in their eyes when they stopped feeling beautiful and instead felt foolish.

In an instant, my embarrassment turned to rage. I hated all those rich white kids with their store-bought costumes. I hated that picture of Black Jesus and all those people who sang so lustily on Sunday mornings. I hated that they tricked me into bringing my beautiful girls into this place. For the past few years, I had been trying to explain to these lovelies that they weren't that different, that we were more similar than not. We were neighbors, we were friends, we were family. But instead, this place—*my church, I had called it my church*—made them feel like Others, just as everyone else did. Although it was a different church, it reminded me of the VBS, of countless other times I had put my refugee friends in a situation where they were the outsiders, and I was the benevolent, clueless insider.

We assessed the situation, stole some stickers when backs were turned, and were rewarded with tiny bags of the cheap candy, Tootsie Rolls and such. I made a decision then to reject what this place had offered us that night and grandly refused the candy. We ushered the girls into the car and drove to the nearest grocery store where we let the girls each pick out a big bag of their favorite candy. Their eyes grew wide and they started to giggle again.

On the way home it was pretty quiet. Eventually Saida mentioned quietly, "All those people were looking at us. Everywhere we go, people are staring." And I felt crushed at having been the one to subject them to this situation and for trying to solve the looks and whispers with my fun-size candy bars. The harvest party was just another experience in alienation, adding to the relentless pounding of a message whispered in their ears all day long: *you are different, you are different, you are different.* I knew that pretty soon they might decide to surround themselves only with those who are different in the same way, different just like them.

While trying to protect my girls from this withdrawal from others, I realized that this is what harvest parties are all about. The church, me and my kind, had become so focused on taking care of our own that we neglect all those who don't conform, who aren't in our club.

I had done the opposite. I had drawn attention to the differences in a misguided attempt to make us all feel good: the girls, to have a good time, and me, to be seen by the church as a good person. I hadn't protected them because I was born and raised in the church, and for me, there was never any risk involved. I belonged too well, was the problem, so I never considered what it might feel like to someone who didn't.

Now, I look back on that night with sadness, as well as awe. Hali, Saida, and Khadija were so brave, so willing to be vulnerable, to extend a relationship to me and my church. Their lives in America consisted of these kinds of interactions over and over again. The stares, the whispers, the confusion. Their bodies never belonged; they always seemed to take up too much space. And yet, when I asked them to come, to enter into my world—filled with people who looked just like me—they did. They came with me to church, but they were the ones who taught me about hospitality, about the courage of opening up your life to the unknown and the foreign, day after day after day.

They were the ones who had no place to be at home in the world, so in the end it is no surprise to me that they are the ones who taught me the most about God and his ways in the world. I would have to leave the churches and Bible colleges, the buildings and institutions I had planned my life around, in order to find that mysterious kingdom. I would have to go to the places Jesus always said he would be. Because I didn't know exactly where Jesus was or what he looked like, but I was starting to get some ideas.

I would find him in the faces that looked so unlike mine.

As a young child, I, like all great missionaries, was eager to take the weight of the world on my shoulders. I pressed my cheek to the rock of the world, the vast and great hordes of unbelievers. What shall I tell them? About Jesus, of course. What would I say? I would figure it out when I got there. The great narratives told around me were primarily of going; there was not much conversation regarding what was to be said.

What they didn't tell me is that it is only the young and the foolhardy who try to convert others. It is the bright-eyed and dewy-skinned who clutch the books that they read, the doctrines lined up just so; they are the ones with all the right answers. Never mind their loneliness and doubts, the fears and the pressure to be a little Christ, to emulate their master without offending as he so often did. They are to do his job better, to convince and plead and wheedle, to have enough faith to do it all.

I tried to do it. I took the words of others—the scriptures, my pastors, my Bible college professors—and I repeated them to anyone around me. It never worked, but that was no bother to me. This was a sign of being a prophet: no one ever listens to you. It never occurred to me what it might be like to receive lessons about death and God and the unbearable weight of existence from a nineteen-year-old girl who was entirely sure of herself. But as I worked with the refugees in my community, with Jamila and her family, the shine of my new missionary life began to wear off, and the heroes I idolized were nowhere around to help me.

Then, when I was nearly thirty, I met Frank Laubach.

You wouldn't know it by his book of letters, but Frank Laubach was a famous missionary. He was a man who sailed off to the Philippines to convert the "Moslems," as they were called then. He wandered around the villages and tried to be useful, tried to talk of God. In the end, his life was celebrated as a success: he pioneered countless literacy programs, brought his knowledge of grassroots educational systems to over one hundred countries, and made the world a better place for the "silent billions" as he called those who had no access to education. He wrote countless books about God and his love; he is the only missionary to be featured on a U.S. Postal Service stamp.

When Frank Laubach was forty-six years old, he wrote a series of letters to his father, detailing a mystical experiment he had recently undertaken. "I want to keep God in my mind always," he wrote, completely sincere, detailing his struggles and triumphs in great detail to his dad. When he was forty-six, Frank Laubach changed. He started walking to the top of a hill, overlooking the town where he had stationed himself, an agent of the Lord most high. He started to will God's presence on the people, to will it in himself the same. His quiet body, quietly sitting, with his mind focused on love emanating out-side of himself toward all those walking below, unaware of how close God really was. He sat on the top of a hill and thought about God's love.

To his own father Frank did not write about any of his

successes; he did not know what he was to become. When I read his book of letters, I imagine myself sitting still and small and overlooking the world above. It feels uncomfortable; it feels more than a bit like heresy. I have been valued for my feet and my hands, and the work that they produce. It is God who sits above and judges and loves equally; it is not my place to sit and catch my breath, to will something that I am not even sure I experience in the first place. Then the real question emerges, the one that has been here all along: What exactly is it that I am trying to convert people into?

I read the letters Frank wrote to his father and think, *He is either a truly happy man, or he is mad.* Does it make a difference what he was? Perhaps it doesn't—the world is littered with saints who walked the razor's edge of sanity. It does matter, however, in our current world, if Laubach in the end made something of himself, if he changed the world in any quantifiable way. For if he hadn't been deemed successful, his book of letters would not have been published at all.

Around the time that Frank wrote of his rapturous experiments in minute-by-minute communion with God, he was busy creating and developing both the first written script in the Moro language and developing a literacy curriculum that would change the world—Each One Teach One, a brilliant strategy that asked the adult literacy learners to commit to teach at least one other person what they themselves had absorbed. How Christian is this? The desire not only to better oneself but also to change the person right next to you—to convert them—to a better way of life. I was surprised, however, when I later read the motivation behind Laubach's transcribing the written language of the Moro people. It was not, as I had originally guessed, so that the people could read and understand the Word of God (a traditional missionary endeavor that I myself had halfheartedly attempted). No, Laubach had noticed how sad the people of the village seemed and had asked them what their troubles were. It seems that many members of the village had to move far away in order to work; without a written form of communication (and long before telephones came) there was simply no way for loved ones to reach out to each other. So Frank determined to find them a way, using literacy. He was determined to help people love each other, just as he was determined to understand for himself how much God loved the world.

When I read his book of letters, I couldn't help but gasp at the commonalities between us: the literacy programs, the unease with the privilege and power we were born into, the emotions oscillating between serene love and a hysterical grief at the world. And so, even though he had been dead and gone for so many years, I decided to write Frank Laubach a letter of my own.

Dear Frank,

I do what you did. I sit next to some of the poorest people in the world, ones whose lives are so different from mine that I don't even bother pretending anymore. We look at sheets of paper, look at the scratches we make together. A few of my students learn. Their eyes track in the right direction, they carefully print the shapes and lines. Most of them do not learn. They sit and they smile at me, they clasp my hand, they want to know how my daughter is doing. Behind their eyes is a cloud of unknowing, the result of traumas stacked up like a pyramid, the current life crises that they ricochet back and forth from. Someone is always losing their housing. Someone is always losing their medical benefits. A child is always sick, or being beaten up at school, or running away. The husbands are always gone, some dead in the war, some dead by sickness, some with another wife, another woman, some trying desperately to get a visa. They are the poor in America, and they are required to go to classes and to work in day-care centers and to sit and stare at pages with me, the teacher. I do not understand what I am supposed to do. I do not understand how complicated the world is, what the lives of my students are like, how hard it is to quiet bodies and minds and go over the vowel sounds one more time.

I am a little hysterical, these days. I am confused by whether I should feel self-righteous or cynical. If I were to write a book of letters to my own father, they would read like the journal of a crazy person, someone who is desperately working for God while still being very unclear on whether or not he loves her. I would love to have my face be placed on a stamp someday, if I am being completely honest. Maybe then, finally, I could be sure I had done some good in the world.

At one point, near the end of the book of letters that you wrote to your own dad, you gave me a glimpse into the fraught undercurrents that belied your modern mystic title. On August 21, 1937, you wrote: "So many of the people here and everywhere seem to have more cramped lives and hopeless minds even than I have. I have been trying to teach a boy to read this afternoon, but his mind seems to be like pouring water into a mosquito net. . . . What a tragedy to live in the world he lives in."

I read that, and I thought: *There it is, the despair I feel on a daily basis.* But the very next line strikes me just as true, even as it veers wildly off course emotionally: "I felt a warm love for the boy." That's all I want.

At times it feels like cramped minds and hopeless lives are all that I am surrounded by. But this is one thought, one fleeting moment in a life that is so full of God and so full of his absence that I can't be trusted to know my own thoughts at any given moment. Like you, I chose this dream of being a missionary, willingly pursued it, throwing myself into the needs I found around me. To my fellow believers I exhort and encourage love and compassion, trotting out the good works that I have done, my stomach sinking like a stone within me. I myself am so small, so ineffective, neither truly happy nor pleasantly mad. I am tired of wanting to be like you.

But I feel compelled to share this with you, as I think you will understand. More often than not, when I least expect it, the warmth of love overwhelms me. It overtakes me as my students rise up, majestically, from their chairs, scraping the floor, sweeping jumbled papers into grimy backpacks. They always grab me, embrace me, and kiss me on both cheeks. Their bracelets jangle against me, and I am swallowed, just for a moment, into their compassion, into their love for me, the distraught and tired do-gooder, the one who cannot face herself if she isn't doing some good for the world. Their love enfolds me. And it reminds me of another, greater, love than this.

You had your hill, the one you hiked to all those years ago, sitting and dwelling with God forever on your mind, being radically transformed by a love that transcends explanation. I have my running route, the place where I slowly pound my feet into the pavement of my neighborhood. I run by the infamous mosque, the one where the boys left and went to Ethiopia and became human bombs, hoping to escape the demons in this world. I run by the asphalt company, breathing in the noxious fumes. I run past the older gentlemen sitting on discarded bucket seats, taking a smoke break. I run up my own hill, up the pedestrian bridge that goes over the highway which slices my neighborhood into two. And I stop, at the peak of the bridge, and look over at my city, at the high-rise apartments where so many of my friends and neighbors and students live.

And Frank: I stop at the top of the bridge, sweaty and tired, almost ready to turn back toward home. I think, *Why not?* There is nothing more to lose, and so much I need to gain. I stand quietly, eyes focused on the thousands of souls that I never could fully see. And I try to be like you, try to pray the love of God on the city. I try to imagine it as an ocean of longing, the beams of the sun transforming into the only presence big enough for all of our needs. And as I pray, I can't help but hope that the tiniest sliver of that light would fall on me as well.

Nostalgia

One year I organized an art class for a bunch of Somali Bantu kids who were desperately bored during spring break. I can't remember all the details because those years were full of well-meaning but chaotic programs and events. Never one to seek out hard work or organization or responsibility, I strangely found myself becoming a party planner for refugee kids, filling in the holes left by a school system that wasn't equipped to deal with preliterate, traumatized children. I put together art classes, homework clubs, field trips, and basketball camps. I would try anything to get them out of their apartments, where they watched dreary PBS cartoons almost nonstop.

By hanging around with Jamila's family, I eventually met the seventeen other Somali Bantu families who had all migrated to a specific low-income apartment complex in my city. The entire complex smelled of goat liver, oil, and ginger. Around every corner you found women buying colorful dresses out of the trunks of cars, men smoking and laughing on the steps, and children shrieking and running and pulling on your legs. They had created their own world in the midst of modernity, and I was happy to spend my free time in Little Somalia.

During that particular spring break, I decided the art class would be a sort of free-form "process" kind of event (i.e., throwing a few crayons and pieces of paper around and calling it good if nobody lost an eye). We all met in the community room of the apartment complex, and I wandered around, keeping my eye on the squirrelliest of the boys and reveling in the din of nonbored children.

I came upon one small boy, age six or seven or eight (it can be so hard to tell, especially as they were assigned birthdays by government officials as part of the resettlement process). While most of the kids were drawing typical square houses with smiling suns and weird, squat stick figures, this little boy had drawn a lion. Dragging something in the dirt. Nonchalantly, I asked, "Nabin, is that a lion?" "Uh huh." "What is that?" I asked, pointing to the smudge in the lion's mouth. Nabin didn't look up. "That's a boy." The din of the room was suddenly replaced with stillness, the sound of my joy being swallowed by horror. "Nabin, did you see this happen?" He is stoic, intent on finishing the picture. Coloring in some more dirt, a few tufts of grass, a sun with no smiley face. He nods his head. A few kids gather around, interested in my stricken face. They snatch the picture out of Nabin's hands. "Ooooh, yeah," they say. "I remember when the boy got eaten." The older ones sense the drama of the moment, the littler ones are confused and quiet. "I remember when the boy got eaten by a lion. My mother would not let us play outside for a week. We just sat inside all day, so boring." They let the paper drop, it floats to the floor. Another volunteer picks it up and we tape it to the wall along with the rest of them, the square houses, the four-petal flowers, mermaid families. One true story, framed by copies of other stories.

The thought came to me that I might be over my head here. An art class, it was becoming increasingly clear, would not be enough.

Around that same time I took a handful of the kids to see a movie in the theater for the first time. We saw *Charlotte's Web*, and the kids would shriek and shout and giggle and talk loudly to each other and to the characters on the screen, and I almost died of mortification. There came a scene where the crow is talking to somebody (a pig? or Charlotte? or some girl? I was too busy shushing children to pay attention), and all the Somali Bantu kids got really quiet. I shrugged it off and enjoyed the peace until I noticed the little girl next to me, Duni, was crying. "What's wrong?" I whispered. She just pointed at the bird on the screen and cried silently. I rubbed her little back and then crept down the aisle until I found Hali, the oldest girl. "Why is Duni crying?" I asked. Hali was looking pretty freaked out herself. "It's the bird," she said, motioning to the crow. "That's the bird that eats the eyes of the dead people." Silence. Crouching awkwardly in the aisle, my mind is racing. "Is that something your mom told you? About the bird?" Hali looks at me strangely. "My mother didn't tell us," she says. "We all see it."

I tell the kids to cover their eyes until the crow flies away, and then we watch a movie about spiders dying and how tragic it is. I can't stop thinking that this movie—a story designed to introduce children to the circle of life concept in an uplifting manner—only succeeded in becoming another grim reminder that there was no margin in their own childhoods, no buffers to keep the unimaginable at bay.

Looking back, it is clear that although I was eager to help them—spiritually, logistically, socially—I was completely unprepared to work with the levels of atrocities, the horror of slavery, war, rape, famine, and death that was their collective history. I was ignorant, enthusiastic, naive, and eventually heartbroken. Art classes, basketball camps, and homework clubs are laughable when viewed through the history of the Somali Bantu. But in my own small way, I was trying to ease their burdens.

Finally, the day that I had been dreading came. The Somali Bantu family I was closest to, Jamila and her girls Hali, Saida, and Khadija, moved again. It was only across town, but factoring in the realities of bus systems, crazy schedules, and a lack of driver's licenses, I knew things would not be the same. I was trained by the past few years of working with refugees that things can change so fast. Diaspora is in the blood. Possessions and apartments and cities are held lightly. People come and go, sometimes finding a better life (but usually finding the same kind of existence in another beige apartment complex). Jamila was always telling me that they were going to move again. I didn't fully believe her until the day I showed up to find their apartment in trash bags again, the only furniture left a gigantic TV that was still blaring some sort of tween sitcom from the Disney channel. But I still refused to believe it.

I had moved into the same apartment complex three years before, confident that we would always be neighbors. Jamila would very rarely talk about the future, and when she did, it was slippery, soluble, not always steeped in fact. "We are moving next week," her girls would tell me, bobbing up and down excitedly. "Our mom told us we will have a yard! And a pool! And our own rooms!" They had absorbed the American dream just like any other cable-watching family. And then, "Our mom said we can go to college!" they would tell me, uncertain even then of what that all meant. "Our mom said we don't have to get married right away," they would inform me nonchalantly as they cooked and cleaned around the house. The longer I knew them, the more I knew not to trust these future-tense statements. For many refugees, the future is a broad and blank place of generalizations, fragments of new dreams buoyed by no connection to past lives. For many refugees, the future is very, very hard to visualize. There is only the inescapable, crushing present, which ultimately leads to a mythological past.

A refugee, for all intents and purposes, is someone who has no past to go back to. And so it makes sense that they idealize it in order to make sense of the present, to have some sort of hope for the future. For many of my Somali Bantu (and Bhutanese, Burmese, and other refugee) friends, their defining characteristic is their nationality. It is no matter that most of them spent the past decade or two in a refugee camp in a different country (or that the majority of their children were born in Kenya, or Nepal, or Thailand). They identify with the country that expelled them, with the country that will never again exist in this world.

But Jamila and her family did move across town, and it could be another state for how difficult it was for me to see them consistently. I was no longer the footloose and fancy-free volunteer: I juggled teaching ESOL at the community college and then tracked the nap schedules of my child. When I did have a few hours to fight the horrible traffic, I made the trek across town. When I would arrive at their new house, sweaty and exhausted, the girls would be languid, bored, glued to the boxy old laptop their mother bought them. Life moved on, little girls became teenagers, and neighbors grew apart. Life had a less hectic tone than it did before. People no longer needed me to go to the welfare offices or to figure out which bag contained sugar and which contained salt. Without Jamila and her family constantly in my life, I started to drift, unmoored, into an ever-smaller circle. I would cry, sitting on my tiny balcony, overlooking my corner of the city. I cried the song of the young: *It's so unfair. Why does everything always have to change?*

A few months later, it was summer in the Pacific Northwest. In our one hot month, the only relief to be found was at the public pool. I slathered sunscreen on the baby and rounded up a few neighbor kids to walk with me—a couple of lovely young ladies from Bhutan, by way of a Nepali refugee camp.

The girls listened attentively, cooed at my baby, and heeded my instructions to only cross at the crosswalk. I marveled at how they listened, how they politely thanked me for walking them to the park.

At the pool, I saw a pack of wild boys, all Somali Bantu, thrashing and jumping and generally behaving in a way that made all the parents pause, sniff, and look around for disciplinarians. There were none there, and I alone knew the boys walked the two miles on their own to the pool. I knew most of their names, both their given names and their secret family names, and I could remember when they were squishy, grinning babies tied to their sisters' backs. Now they are long and lean and loud, swarming in large groups at the kiddie pool. I saw the lifeguards shrill the whistle and talk sternly, I watched the boys laugh and confidently ignore. I put on my sunglasses and stretched out in the sun. I pretended I didn't know any of them and absolved myself of all responsibility. The Bhutanese girls slowly twirled in their corner of the pool, playing quiet games and talking about school drama. This felt like a metaphor for something.

A few years previously, I was the guardian of those wild packs of kids, the eager volunteer. I would have made a big show of talking to the boys, hovering and helpful, stern when I needed to be, setting good boundaries. A part of me loved the stares I got, tramping about this city with all the colorful kids in tow. In the beginning, when there was so much tangible need, I felt gratified to be a part of making their present more bearable. It was only later I realized that the present never mattered much to them, and I never had quite the starring role I thought I did.

It is hard for me to give up on myself, on my own future dreams that hinge on me saving people, converting others, changing all the wrongs into rights. I have wild thoughts like,

If I just could have done more—more homework clubs, job educa-tion courses, Jesus film showings, prayer times—then I could have done something. Then maybe my friends would not be moving away. People I adore would not get lost in violence, or get mar-ried at age fifteen, or be crushed by debt the rest of their lives. In the weird way that nostalgia works, I am casting myself as a hero of sorts in our narratives. But underneath my histrionics is the unsettling reality that I am not needed anymore, and if I am, then I don't have the strength to do it. All of us are trying to forge on in a world that is reluctant to give up the space, to make a place for us wanderers. I am finding that I am nostalgic for something that never even happened. I long for the world where I was saving everybody and where everybody was being saved—where the truth of my worth, my calling, my work was to save these families. And even though I know this alternate world created out of nostalgia never even existed, I still miss it so.

The Do-Gooder

A few years after those crazy, chaotic early years, I no longer had the youthful enthusiasm and optimism to run my own homework club anymore, but I still volunteered at one from time to time. We now lived in another low-income neighborhood, a place where the youth groups come on spring break. I saw them prayer walking, prayer giggling, prayer flirting up and down my somewhat grimy streets. I heard them, and I was transported back to the previous summer, when the churches flocked into the neighborhood parks, put up awnings, cooked a meal, gave a message. People wandered around in T-shirts that said "Bringing Good to the 'Hood." I went there a few times with my daughter, happy to eat a free chicken dinner. But I stared at the people running around in their lime-green T-shirts, and I was confused. I forgot, for a moment, that I lived in the 'hood. Thanks for the reminder. I forgot, for a moment, that there was no good here until you showed up with your microphones and chicken dinners and matchy-matchy shirts. Thank you, thank you for *bringing it,* I shook my head slowly, and wiped the sauce off my daughter's fingers. I felt sorry for the do-gooders, to whom I am now willing to assign positive, if ill-advised, intent. I felt bad for them, not being as enlightened and humble and *missional* as I was. I ate my free chicken dinner, on the dime of the large church a few blocks and a million years away from what goes on in this park, and I felt smug.

I was still an outsider, but at least I had a couple of years of living with my neighbors in mind under my belt. I was probably doing everything badly, but others would probably do it worse. The problem was that, I too, in my heart of hearts, still believed that I was bringing good to the 'hood. I had just learned to not put it on a T-shirt anymore.

I have some friends who have been living the most incredibly quiet, miraculous lives you ever did see. They live in the midst of the most diverse neighborhood in all of America. They have lived here for decades; they hang out with the people that Jesus hung out with in the Bible, people that seem extremely exotic to someone like me: prostitutes, pawn collectors, people somewhere in the process of recovery, the chronically unemployed. They have seen miracles happen, to be sure, in the people they have hung out with. They have testimonies that I would have longed to claim for my own when I was younger—Jesus saving people from drugs and promiscuity and family problems. But they have also stuck around long enough for the stories to get shiny with age, to crack at the seams. They have watched as people's testimonies went up and down the scales, as addictions and families and lies turned the static conversions into actual lives. They have seen stories as they really are: long-term and full of miracles and crushing disappointments, a constant tale of being saved and relapsing back into ourselves.

But nobody wants to be this couple. Nobody wants to hang out in the bad neighborhoods for decades. The problems seem to get more overwhelming, the longer you stay. The easy paint jobs got taken, the kids already ate your snacks and heard the stories you had prepared for them, your friend never followed up on the job interview you arranged for him. The cosmetic fixes have all been applied, and people still go home to abuse and neglect, with empty bellies and numbed hearts. If you stay long enough you will learn just enough about the brokenness of the world that you will feel completely powerless, mired in your own brokenness and doubting God more often than you care to admit.

It is easier to leave right after the prayers are prayed, right after somebody meets Jesus, while the tears are still fresh and the hope is solid enough to cut with a knife. While everyone is doing okay, taking pictures that we can take home and cling to, framing the ones where everyone is smiling. We, the do-gooders, stay for a short while, because we crave the knowledge that we have done something of value in the world. And we leave before we have a chance to see how poor in relationships we really are.

I've done this do-gooder work for years now, what I thought were valiant, honorable efforts, but what was more often than not just a roundabout way of trying to come to terms with the inequalities in our world. And I've learned how dipping our toes in the pool of humanity—going and helping and doing—actually impoverishes and deceives us. For a few days, weeks, and months, we allow ourselves to see the other side. We swing from the ends of helplessness to arrogance, back and forth. We become zealots, lovers, missionaries, and activists. We read articles, pause and let the words sink in, stare at the pictures until they are burned into our brains. And then we forget. We always forget—that comforting, calming, after-effect of our world. No one can live in that tension forever, and soon enough you will be able to forget.

In the throes of it, overwhelmed by the needs of our refugee neighbors, I asked everyone I knew to help me just to spread the burden around a bit. Some people came—friends from church and Bible college mostly. My husband and I pleaded with our friends, drove them downtown to the low-income apartment complexes, and watched their eyes grow wide as they entered into that other world. The kids attacked these newcomers, ferocious in their desire for love and affirmation, clinging to every limb, snatching up every focused gaze. I ran around the edges, one eye on the troublemakers, pleased at the connections I was making between my two worlds. I watched as my friends would laugh and tutor and hug their little homework buddies, snap pictures on their cell phones, and post the images later that same day to Facebook. "Me and my buddy Mohammed!!!!," the album would say, filled with images of smiles so wide you thought they would break.

And then, week after week, our friends stopped coming. They didn't feel good, they got really busy, they just plain forgot. The kids, packed inside the bare community room, watching the winter rain fall down, pressed their faces against the windows, waiting for their new best friends to come back. But in the end, life always got the best of them, my good-hearted, flaky friends. And they never got to see the faces of the continually disappointed, the way they set their shoulders, how they tried harder the next time to get this volunteer to like them, to pay attention to them, to stick around longer than a month or so.

When I first started hanging out with my refugee friends, I could see how they had changed me. They had revealed to me the darker truths behind the myth of the American dream. I was mesmerized by the poverty I saw and astounded by the resilience and relational strengths contained therein. I assumed other people would love these sorts of surprising friendships, so I tried to get others to come with me. I wanted to see them converted in front of my eyes as well.

But eventually, my enthusiasm to see others join in the work was replaced with a gradual sense of protecting my friends that we were working with. My husband and I hung around long enough to see what it does to communities when they are targeted, time and time again, for short-term, feel-good projects. We hung around long enough to feel the pain of abandonment, the shame of being a project, the vulnerability it feels to have someone come, smile, call you their best friend, snap a picture, and leave. So eventually, we stopped inviting people to come and volunteer at all. The cost, it turns out, was too great. The desire to do good was not enough, and we were starting to see how it could actually do more harm in the long term.

A few years after I first met them, I had Saida and Khadija over for a sleepover. Like the good little mentor that I was, I talked about future plans for college, and how disappointed I was by the misogyny found in so much popular rap, how organized sports for girls were so amazing and empowering. Saida, then age fourteen, started to interrupt me, becoming uncharacteristically eager to talk—mainly about a boy she met on the Internet, and how badly she wanted to get married. I felt my jaw tighten and my breathing become faster. But for once, I stopped myself before I could blossom into full-blown lecture mode. As Saida jabbered to me in the kitchen while we made cookies, I decided to simply listen for once. I asked a couple of questions, but for the most part she rambled on and on about how cute and nice this (much older) boy was. I looked at her little sister Khadija, age thirteen, who was sitting at the table and busy aggravating my toddler.

"Khadija," I said. "Do you want to get married too? Or do you want to go to college?" I could see her stretch her long arms across the table, tickling the baby's toes.

"Ummmmmm," she drew out her answer dramatically. "Yeah, I guess I want to go to college." She wasn't very convincing. I decided right then and there to stop pretending, to stop playacting as though I were the good volunteer and they were the impressionable and moldable young girls in this story. I decided to play it straight.

"Khadija," I said, "do you know any Somali Bantu girls that have ever gone to college?" I could hear her pause, stop fidgeting for one second. And then she laughed. "No, I don't know anybody."

I somewhat grimly went on: "Do you really think you are going to go to college?" She answered much too quickly, with a decisiveness that made me want to curl up and cry. "No, I don't think so. That is just something we tell you."

I sighed, shook my head, and turned up the terrible Christian rap I play as a compromise that none of us liked. And later, I replayed the conversation over and over in my head. I wondered why I wasn't more upset, more up in arms about what I saw as an issue of social justice. The Somali Bantu girls I knew were getting married at younger and younger ages, entering a patriarchal and polygamous system where they will be expected to have lots of babies and cook three times a day. From the first day I met them, I had made it a goal of mine to see these girls through to college. Now, it looked like I might have to put those dreams away to die. But the biggest emotion I felt was relief: for the first time it felt like we were finally being honest with each other.

Once I thought I was going to save everybody. Through Jesus's love and homework help, art projects and good literature, church activities and the sheer force of my goodwill. This way of framing life points to the dangerous thinking of the savior complex: I am the sun, and everybody else is just a moon. But of course, I don't shine so brightly in anyone else's eyes, and I am learning this slowly.

The tendency to make these girls props is still strong: part of me wants to petition child protection services or write a journalistic exposé of polygamy or do a self-esteem workshop. But the reality is that the best way to humanize an issue is to actually be involved in it. If the girls remained mere props in my story, I would bluster and bully until they slipped away, retreating to be with people who thought just like them. I would be able to indulge in the luxury of outrage and wallow in the affront to my altruistic goals. I would probably give up, washing my hands of a complicated situation and consoling myself with the thought that I really had tried my hardest.

But when I become the bit part, the background player in a much larger saga, I find my true role, which is this: to swallow my own impulse to save and to focus on the long game. To be a friend, the truest form of advocacy there is. To listen to them talk about their boyfriends or how much they love Chris Brown or plan their weddings. This is the new reality, and I have to work with it. Love God, love your neighbor, Jesus said, a perfect sound bite for the ages. But did Christ know how complicated my neighbors were? How hard they were to love sometimes? How much easier it is to surround myself with people who look and think and act like me, to love only myself? Yes, yes, yes, he does, but he is polite and firm in his response. A messy, present, incarnational love is the simplest and hardest call of all, the call that all of us were created to follow.

And this is how I find myself offering to bake the damn wedding cake.

3

Depression and Culture Shock

The Wedding

I still had many savior complex daydreams, but I tried to fight them back. And as the troubles of my refugee friends piled high around me, I started to sense new questions emerging. I was finding the kingdom in all of these little pockets, but it was never enough. There were too few miracles to go around, and the small doubts started to grow in me. Maybe I wasn't enough, maybe I was doing it all wrong, maybe God was just a teensy bit blind up there in the sky. In a way, I sure hoped he was. It would answer so many of my questions.

We were in the car when Hali asked me to do the makeup at her wedding. She was a junior in high school. She was gorgeous, polite, and severe when things didn't please her. For the past four years we had plotted her path through the world: make it through the hell that is high school, go to college, and then get married (she said she wanted to be an ESOL teacher, a touch I liked since that is exactly what I became). And then—her two younger sisters let the news about the out-of-state boyfriend and the wedding slip. I asked too many questions, and my voice got all high-pitched. Then I lost her, watched her slip away from me in all the tiny ways.

In the car, staring out the window and fiddling with her MP3 player, she asked me to do the makeup. "I will give you the money, and then you can bring it on the day," she told me. I asked her why we couldn't just buy it together and she would keep it. "I am not supposed to have anything when I get married," she said. "My husband will take care of me then, buy me anything I need." As I tried to absorb this information she casually added: "Oh, and can you make me the big cake too? Nobody else has ever had this, and I want it." I said yes immediately, desperate for any tenuous connection to this girl and her wedding, not ready to say goodbye.

We were at the cake-decorating store, buying supplies for the big event. I knew we would stick out, as we always do: the frazzled volunteer with the three girls in head scarves trailing behind, touching everything in sight. I had to remember to breathe deeply and that people were watching us closely. We went up to the counter, and a woman in her midthirties helped us, kindly explaining things like what size cake pans would fit in my oven and how many layers would be feasible. And then her eyes flicked over to Hali, who was looking at the displays of confectionery roses, dreaming of what her cake was going to look like. "Is it her wedding?" the woman at the counter asked me. I nodded. She edged closer to Hali, leaning her bosom on the glass countertop. "Honey," she said, firm and full of kindness, speaking with an intimacy I could only dream of having with Hali. "You are much too young to get married."

Hali looked at her, large brown eyes clear as could be. "Oh, I know." She said, and smiled wide.

We were watching *High School Musical* together for the billionth time, when Hali suddenly asked me to rewind a scene. I did, and we watched as the mousy girl (messy brown bun, glasses) who plays the piano get her day in the sun. During the finale of the film, where the kids put on the musical in question, she is transformed. Sitting down at the piano wearing a bowler hat and vest, she slowly rises. She takes off her hat and shakes her head, causing a cascading wave of luxurious hair. She sings, and then you notice her glasses are gone, she is wearing makeup, and everyone is all, like, "Hey! That girl is pretty!," and she looks very pleased.

We watched it over and over again, at Hali's insistence. She sat forward in her chair, immersed in the modern fairy tale of believing in yourself. Hali, the girl who was covered from head to toe in fabric, head scarf dutifully on, who was normally forbidden from wearing makeup at all. And I knew she wanted a chance, just like that girl in the movie, to shake her hair out in front of everyone. To be transformed, to have one song-and-dance number be all about her.

My apartment was covered in flour, and there were large, lopsided cakes covering my kitchen table. The baby was up from her nap early, irritated at being plunked in her high chair while I tried to smush pieces together to create some semblance of a three-tiered monstrosity.

While the baby waved her little arms and gnashed her four teeth like a little tyrannosaur, I became despondent over the state of my cake. It looked positively "Seussical," but not in a whimsical way. I smeared on the frosting I bought at the Hispanic market, the thick, unsweet shaving-cream-like frosting that the immigrants and refugees in my life have always served me. I smeared it on and hoped for the best. I piped on the purple roses (Hali's favorite color) and fed the baby more Cheerios, and I topped it off with the gaudiest plastic-and-lace heart you have ever seen.

The late-afternoon light was streaming in yellow, the wedding only hours away. I eyed the cake critically, despairing at all the flaws. And then I laid down in the middle of my living room, and shut my eyes. The cake really was the least of my worries.

One floor below my apartment, Hali and her bridal party (all fifteen to sixteen years old) were getting ready. I saw her, fresh from the hair salon, covered in bridal henna. Her hair was smooth, black, and shiny. It was the one day in her life she didn't have to wear the head scarf. I felt teary, parental, overwhelmed.

My unflappable friend Julia, to whom I had outsourced the makeup gig, was surrounded by teenage girls. Julia was no stranger to hanging out with gaggles of refugees and brought a calm and firm presence to the chaos of the room. The bridal party was a sassy, high-pitched bundle of nervous energy. Like being in a debutante ball, being a bridesmaid signaled they were ripe for marriage themselves. They drank can after can of Orange Fanta and admired the henna on their hands. They played hip-hop music videos, yelled into cell phones, and told Julia to put on more and more and more eye makeup. I hovered, completely useless at beautifying rituals but just trying to be a part of the process. I printed off directions to the wedding site and handed them out to the men downstairs, I took pictures while the girls posed, and I turned off the rap music when it became unspeakably crass (I am very, very good at Shutting Things Down).

We got the phone call that it was time to go to the ceremony, and we all gathered to give Hali advice. She looked exceedingly calm, like she had withdrawn almost completely inside of herself. I realized that for once in my life, I didn't have any advice to give her.

The music at the wedding was so loud that the speakers had long ago died, and you could hear metal bits buzzing about. Somali Bantus from all over the West Coast were there, congregating in front of the Russian dance studio where the celebration was to take place and talking loudly over the fuzzed-out bass that was spilling from inside. Julia and I conscripted several teenage boys to help us carry in the cake, and I don't know what got more stares: that confectionery masterpiece or the sight of two white girls at the wedding.

To distract myself from the emotions lying near the surface I switched into cultural anthropologist mode, making mental notes about the fabulous dresses and all the rituals I didn't understand. The room was large and surrounded by mirrors, with a few tables off to the side piled high with speakers and other DJ equipment. There were chairs hugging the walls, and in the middle of the room was a large circle of women, dancing slowly, slowly, slowly around the room. They were women of all ages, some with babies strapped to their backs, twirling and shuffling and generally just having a good time.

I camped out on the sidelines with Julia, ears aching and head throbbing and with a large lump in my throat. I was grateful that it was too loud to talk; I wouldn't have known what to say.

After what seemed like hours of waiting, we were all ushered outside again to watch as the bride and groom held hands, which someone told us meant they were now married. We all followed them inside waving banners in the air, the women yelling and trilling at the top of their lungs. Then the entire bridal party did something like one hundred laps around the little room, dancing slow as molasses, everyone looking young and beautiful and never taking their eyes off the floor. I stared at the groom, tall and thin, dressed in a gray suit and never taking off his sunglasses. I tried to think kind thoughts, to be an optimistic person for once in my life.

After several hours of this, the bride and her girls were ushered off to do a complicated dress change. I was up way past my bedtime, needing to get home to relieve the babysitter. I asked when the cake would be cut and was told it would happen at the end of the wedding. Well, when will that be? "Oh, 4 or 5 in the morning." I decided to leave, right then and there.

I tried to find Hali in the crush of people surrounding her. Her sisters found me, breathless with the excitement of it all, faces covered in makeup that was obviously applied by someone not as talented as Julia. They told me that things had changed, that Hali was moving to the East Coast instead of Seattle, that she had just been told herself. I shouted at the girls over the din. "When is she moving? Next week?" No, they told me. She is leaving tomorrow.

I frantically pushed through people until I found Hali and her pack of girls in a small changing room. She had warned me beforehand that she wouldn't be able to talk to me at the wedding, that I shouldn't be worried by how sad she looked.

She had explained that in her culture it would be disrespectful to look happy on her wedding day—she was, after all, leaving her family behind. I found her, in a beautiful dark-green dress that looked like a sari, and clutched her wrist. "Hali," I said, "I love you." I swallowed, and then lied through my teeth: "I am so happy for you." She nodded her head. I rushed on, talking fast and close to her ear.

"I want you to know that you can always call me. If you ever, *ever* need anything, please call me. I will always be here." Her eyes looked up at me and she nodded, and then she was led away to continue the dancing, side by side with the man she had only met twice in real life.

The children were all crowded around the cake, staring with wide eyes at all that frosting, taking little licks when they thought no one was watching. Babies were sleeping in chairs, on the floor, on their mothers' backs. The music kept pulsing, one song blending into another, and the women kept dancing. Julia and I snuck out the back door, and I got my last look at Hali, so gorgeous and young, having her day in the sun, and a feeling worse than sadness started creeping in.

I thought about the countless conversations about colleges and careers, the introduction of Disney preteen media and "follow your dreams" mantras, the talks about Jesus and how much he loves and values women, my harping on equitable marriages, on waiting to have children, on finishing high school. As I drove away from the wedding, there was only one thought in my head: What if I had made everything worse?

Abdi, Jamila's husband, was dying. Several years ago I was informed that all he wanted was to wash in the ocean before he died.

He had been dying ever since I first met him, that grand old man of the apartment complex, dressed in pristine clothes and carrying a distinguished cane. He could be both severe and effusive within a matter of seconds, and I was slightly terrified of him. He would always rise when I entered a room and extend his hand for me to clasp. He was missing a finger on his right hand, which I tried never to stare at. He taught me how to do the proper greetings: *As-Salaam Alaikum. Wa-Alaikum Salaam.*

I could never really tell for sure what he had. Tuberculosis, I had heard. I spent so much time with the family that I needed shots to protect against TB and ended up testing *slightly* positive for it at my Bible college (minor heart attacks all around). The other disease is what seemed to be truly killing him, parasites he got from Africa and the well-meaning American doctors giving him medications that had started to liquefy his internal organs. His skin turned gray, he lost what little weight he had, and the whites of his eyes glowed a neon yellow.

He was shipped off to the Midwest for three months, where the doctors evidently know a little more about tropical diseases. I was worried it was the last time I would ever see him, but Abdi came back as fresh as I had ever seen him, yelling at all of us to go fetch him some food and then smiling broadly at us, like some benevolent dictator and his clueless subjects.

Life went on for a year. Abdi lived his life with relish, always sadly frowning and telling me he was dying, yet actively indulging in every pleasure his doctors had strictly forbidden: smoking a pipe on the front steps, eating spicy hot Cheetos delicately, one at a time, drinking a covert beer now and then.

And then I was informed by Hali, his oldest daughter, that he wanted to go to the ocean and wash in it before he died. Of course, I accepted the request: you never disobey a dying man.

My friend Jan, the one who first introduced me to the Somali community, volunteered to drive us all to the coast in her beat-up Toyota Corolla. Abdi sat in the front seat, wearing a traditional tunic and cap with the cane between his legs. I sat squished in the middle seat between Abdi's wife (Jamila) and his best friend (Ali). It was very hot in that tiny little car, and it was a two-hour drive to the beach. Jan had purchased some Somali praise music, a covert way of trying to convert our dear friends, and it was all cheap electronic devices and tinny sounds. I found myself happily breathing in the smells of sweat, pretending like I was in Africa. In that moment, it didn't seem so implausible.

We got to the beach and stopped to survey the next challenge. The entire way over I had been so busy praying for everybody that I forgot what the Pacific Northwest coast is like in June: cold. Blustery, gray, and cold. We used the public restrooms and then sat in the car eating boiled corn on the cob that they brought in plastic bags, trying to gain the strength to go out into the wild. The mood turned somber; everyone was quiet as we stared at the gray, white-tipped water. I tried to explain how truly frigid the water would be, using the few words of their language I knew. But Abdi had a look of determination in his eyes and ordered us out of the car. We trudged down the dunes and started making the long trek out to the water. As the wind brought tears to my eyes, I had a sudden thought: *Oh my gosh. If he goes in the water, he'll die of pneumonia. I. Am. Going. To. Kill. Abdi.* I turned around to wave my arms and warn them all, but what I saw stopped me short.

There was Abdi, stripped down to his boxers, staring solemnly at the sea. He was emaciated, tired, hanging on to his cane for dear life. His wife and best friend had stopped walking; we were all staring at Abdi. And he himself was having a staring contest with somebody: Allah, the ocean, himself.

I couldn't breathe, couldn't watch as he stepped into the ice-cold water. I turned my back. Abdi muttered something to himself. I imagined trying to explain his imminent pneumonia to the volunteer organization, cursing myself for getting into this mess. And then I heard the peals of laughter.

I turned back around, and Jamila and Ali were doubled over in laughter, hysterical to the point of tears. Abdi was slowly putting his clothes back on, muttering to himself. "He says it's too cold," Ali gasped, pantomiming Abdi putting one toe in the ocean and then jumping back with a shriek. "He says it's too cold," Ali said, wiping tears from his eyes, "and he wants to go back home."

And that was that.

Unbeknownst to me, they had come prepared for this scenario, filling up the trunk with all sorts of empty milk cartons and detergent bottles. We scooped up as much of the water as we could manage, and drove it home. They later told me that they heated it up on the stove and then dumped it in the bathtub. So Abdi did get his wish, in the end.

On the way home, all three of us fell asleep in the backseat, heads lolling on one another. I woke up, as disoriented and peaceful as a child. I looked around me, the heads of Jamila and Ali resting on my shoulders, Abdi stretched out as much as he could in the front seat. The closeness to it all astounded me. I was young and healthy, and life seemed to stretch ever out in front of me, ready to be saved, ripe for the harvest. I did not know how to prepare for death and sickness and sadness because I did not really think any of those things could ever happen to me.

There is an old spiritual song that goes like this: "wade in the water, wade in the water children, wade in the water, God's gonna trouble the waters." It gets stuck in your head like a funeral dirge, slow and solemn. I heard it later in my life, and I could not let the song go.

Jesus, the Bible tells us, was a refugee. That he would so easily be able to identify with the life experiences of my friends, of Abdi and Jamila and Ali, makes me ache. He experienced many of the same sorrows, running from power-hungry people and experiencing losses of life and culture and home. And he came to deliver people, to heal and restore and bring justice, and to show us that we cannot prove ourselves worthy to God; we are simply his beloved children in the end.

The Bible tells the story in John 5 of Jesus coming to the pool of Bethesda, a place where there was a great multitude of sick people—the paralyzed, the chronically ill, the blind. All of these people in various stages of dying hung out by the pool because they wanted to be well. The Bible tells of a strange, mysterious angel who would come every so often and stir up the waters with his wings; when that happened, the sick and the sad would rush to plunge into the water, to be healed by the touch of God. But one day it is Jesus who goes there, the real-life messenger of God, and he sees a man who has waited nearly four decades to go into the waters and come out new. Jesus asks the most obvious question. Jesus asks the sick man: "Do you want to be made well?" The man answers that he has tried for years to get down to the water whenever it gets muddled, but that others always get to it first. Jesus looks at him and tells him to rise up and walk, and then the Bible tells us that this is exactly what the man did.

I imagine the man just staring at Jesus, then looking around at the thousands of gray souls surrounding him, arms outstretched toward the water, eyes looking high in the sky for a miracle to touch down. Everybody wanting to wade in the water, wanting to be born again, born into different bodies, a different life.

In the car on the way home from the beach, my arms were pinned to my sides by the friends sleeping on either side of me. So when I started to cry big, fat tears, they just rolled right on down my face. I cried because I knew that Jesus understood what it meant when somebody wanted to go wash in the ocean before they died. I cried because I knew that even as I had remained unaware of the masses of the sick and the dying of the world, knowing nothing about the horror and the atrocities and the injustice, Jesus was not. He, a stateless wanderer himself, carried the broken with him wherever he went. He understood their lives of pain and suffering, and he ached with love for the world. But still, the truth remained: most of the people at the pool of Bethesda waded into that water, and they came out the same.

Abdi seemed to rally after that trip. Perhaps the salty ocean water really was restorative. Life went on as normal, or as normal as it was back then. He was still in and out of the hospital, and many of my afternoons were spent ferrying various children and spouses back and forth to his hospital room, delivering meals of cold boiled potatoes and goat meat, since he refused to eat the American food.

One day, about five months after the beach trip, I took his three daughters to visit him during one such occasion. He was sitting upright in his bed when we went in, his eyes as clear as I had ever seen them, papers spread messily all over his bed. When we came in, he announced that he wanted to read us a story.

That sly fox. For the past year or so, Abdi had been learning to read and write in his own language. This was a recent phenomenon because until that year his language hadn't ever been written down. During his years in Somalia, he was denied access to education, and so this was his first experience with being literate in any language. Someone—I didn't know who—had been teaching him to read and write in his brand-new language.

He picked up several of the papers and started to read, slowly and haltingly, sometimes saying the same word three or four times. The pride in his work was palpable. I didn't even need Hali to translate it for me; I knew he was reading the story of his life. The hard times in Somalia, the war, the deaths, the fighting. Fleeing to Kenya, and the experiences of the camps. I heard the names of his children, and he read them painstakingly slowly, savoring the syllables. Then he read about coming to America and being happy, and finally, of meeting me and Jan. When he finished and looked up with those clear eyes, I burst into clapping. He seemed pleased, and paused, and then decided to read the story again. And again.

I didn't know it then, but that was the last time I would ever see Abdi. He read that story as many times as we could take it, his daughters bored and kicking the edges of the bed by the time we left. He ate his cold boiled potatoes and complained bitterly about the hospital food. He was modest in the face of my effusive compliments on his writing achievements, but I could see that deep down he was flushed with pride.

A few days later, he died of complications from his diseases.

At the time, I am ashamed to say, I was pleased that I made it into the glorious, chaotic, painful story that was his life. Later, months later, I asked his daughters if they had saved the story that he had written, his first and last. No one knew where it was. No one can even tell me where he was buried.

He was a poor, uneducated refugee. Nobody cared when he was young and everyone around him was dying; nobody cared when his farms were burned and he almost starved to death on the journey to a refugee camp. And certainly nobody seemed to care much when he arrived here, penniless and sick and with absolutely nowhere else to go.

Where was his deliverer? I wanted to ask. Why was the kingdom, as Bob Dylan so eloquently put it, such a slow train coming? While God was busy waiting for the perfect time to restore everything, people like Abdi lived and suffered and died almost in anonymity.

I couldn't find the right answers in my religion or my scriptures anymore, even though I had been trained to look for them. Instead, all I could find was comfort, a sense of a God who understood my questions and sorrows, a God who could identify with Abdi and his life even when I could not. I also was blessed by my short time with Abdi. I was privileged to meet him, share food with him, drink chai, and listen to his stories. I knew the nickname he had for his middle daughter, the one that roughly translated to "beautiful," how it made her round face flush. I knew he was stern and just. I knew how he waved his cane in the air when he had a good point to make. I knew he only liked his wife's cooking and how proud he was of his only living son. I knew that even though I could not identify with nearly any aspect of his life, I knew someone who could. I had been changed by Abdi's life, and I will carry him with me always. He was like an angel to me, the one to muddy the waters I had always thought were so clear. Abdi, and his entire family, pointed out all the ways I was really paralyzed by indifference and selfishness. They revealed to me the human cost of a very unjust world. But more than anything, it seems to me now, Abdi was a messenger of God himself, asking me the most important question of all: Did I want to be well?

The Woes

In the beginning, I thought only about the blessings that Jesus talked about in his kingdom. I only thought about surrounding myself with those who could see the good things of God: the poor, the sick, the sad, the oppressed. I was doing my work with these people. I was living with them, eating with them, taking them to appointments, and teaching them English. I did not think about the other side. I did not think about the other things that Jesus said: woe to you who are rich, woe to you who are well fed, woe to you who laugh now, woe to you when all people speak well of you. Woe to you, because in the end you shall lose it all.

One time, at my church, I went to the front and stood up by the altar. On the screen behind me I put up a picture of a boy. He was lying on a woven mat, his every bone and rib visible. His skin was dark, his hair short and patchy. He was near death, his eyes focused beyond the picture, beyond the pale of this world. The picture was from Somalia, a week old at most. Entire regions in East Africa were experiencing droughts that would not be relieved for years, experts were saying. I put the picture up, large and excruciating on that white screen. I stared out at the congregation, chin held high as I heard the gasps and starts. I talked about the famine, and I urged people to pray. Pray for water, pray for the people, pray for the boy in the picture. Look hard, I told them, look long and hard at this boy. Every second we long to look away, but I am begging you not to just this once.

I put up that picture, and I watched the audience shift and squirm. If I could have, I would have made the picture as big as the entire podium, inescapable for us all. I watched as people became uncomfortable, until a few eyes shone wet with tears. And a small, hard knot in me was pleased; I wasn't the only one terrified of the reality of a world where this little boy was dying while we sat full and fed in the house of God.

I don't know what day of the week I was born on, but I am willing to bet it was on a Wednesday. I am a child of woe, and always have been. Whenever I have become aware of injustice in the world, I have always wanted others to experience it with me.

Another time, at my sister's birthday, there were a few of us gathered in a relaxed circle, drinks and appetizers balanced precariously in hands. My older sister is gorgeous, talented, and driven—I have always been simultaneously awed by and terrified of her. She knows how to throw a party, that one, and her own birthday was no exception. Everything was perfect. Her friends, too, were all good looking, artistic, kind, and creative. We were talking about heaven knows what—sports, I suppose, or television—when apropos of nothing, I start talking about the famine in East Africa.

My audience is captive, and they are people who are very much occupied with complicated structural nuances in the social sphere, people who are trying to live and work and make something meaningful of it all. They know how to enjoy life, and they also know the nagging ennui that haunts us all. I tell them, the people close enough to hear my voice, about the reality of what the earth is like, halfway around the world from us. I paint a picture of a world where the rain does not come, where nothing can grow and people cannot leave, where God, like the great gray clouds that are so desperately needed, seems to have disappeared. I tell them what happens when the rains don't come and the crops fail. First, I say, the animals die—the cattle, the sheep, the livelihoods. Next, it is the infants, followed by the children. The women are next, until finally, you are left with the men. "The men are always the last to go," I say, "the last survivors." The implicit truth in this—a blatant hierarchy of survival in society at its most gruesome—is astounding to me. I expect others to agree with me, to want to gnaw on this same worrisome truth that I cannot let go: the cattle, the babies, the children, the mothers.

The circle drifts out from me, concentric ripples of unease, then forgetfulness, then light and slow laughter. My husband, eating his snacks from a small paper plate in the corner, comes over and puts his arm around me. "You know," he says, trying to be kind. "That was a little intense for party conversation."

"I know," I say, and head back into the kitchen. Refilling plates, changing gears, plunging once more into the only world that was real for us, forgetting all others.

But I am only pretending to forget. The woes are starting to never leave my mind, and I am so very tired of them.

I see a tweet from some aid organization promoted to the top of my feed. It is something about preventable diseases, something about Africa, I think, something about children dying of diarrhea. I see it, but I don't really understand what it is saying. Is that really something that kills people in this day and age? My eyes skim the tweet. I click over to the seven other tabs open on my screen, off to view enviable lives of fine food and wine and adorable toddlers, off to measure my life compared to others who are basically strangers, yet who all look and act and talk like me, were raised like me, are similar to me. I spend far too much time reading the status updates of people I don't care anything about or feeling jealous of people I have never met. My child wakes up from her nap, cranky and with sweaty hair stuck to her cheeks. I close the laptop, shake the cobwebs out of my brain, and turn back into the mom that I am.

Later that week, I am at the community library, a few blocks from my apartment. A brightly colored basement with world maps and student pictures tacked to the walls. I am tutoring people in English. I do this once a week, a way to remind myself that I am a teacher, that I know things other than the words to "Twinkle, Twinkle, Little Star." I do this to get out of my stuffy apartment, to interact with adults, and to cozy up to my amazing, eclectic, diverse neighborhood. My little corner library, packed to the gills with people: people checking Facebook, watching rap videos on the computer, snoring in the comfiest chairs, waiting for the next bus. My library has the lowest circulation rates in the county; nobody comes there to read—everyone comes to be a part of something bigger.

I see a few of the same students, week after week, but one of the best parts about the tutoring gig is getting to meet new people. The majority of the students are Somali, a culture with which I am slightly in love, people who make me feel comfortable. The women all wear long hijabs in this neighborhood, dark purple or green or the standard-issue black. Their fingers, long and brown, sometimes covered in henna, are often dripping with jewelry, gold and gleaming. Today, I am working with two women, reading some story about going to the grocery store. After we have painstakingly sounded out words for a good hour, the tutoring lulls into an actual conversation, turning, as always, to our families.

They are pleased to hear I have a child. "*Mashallah*!" they say, brightening at this commonality. "How old is she?" "Two," I say, waiting for what comes next. "You will have more?" the women ask, always, some of them pushing me to drop a number—do I want three, four, five, or more? The answer, of course, is much more complicated for me, with my history of traumatic birth and the prognosis that it could likely happen again. So when the women ask (and they always do) about more and more and more babies, I respond with a serene and spiritual *Inshallah* (if God wills), putting my palms piously up to heaven. This always shuts them up, makes them laugh, clasp my arm, and smile. "Inshallah," they agree. Everything is determined by the will of God.

They tell me about their families. One woman, on my right, has five children. The other, on my left, has seven. One has five boys, the other five boys and two girls. I am exclaiming over the similarities (five boys! Mashallah!), when suddenly the woman on my right says something very quietly. I don't quite catch it, and ask her to repeat herself. "I had two girls as well," she says, eyes focused on the paper in front of her. "I had five boys and two girls, too," she says. "But the girls died," she says, her voice even. "They died in Africa, one when she was a baby, the other when she was two."

The basement gets very small and still around us, the three of us sitting at the table. I express my sorrow, she acknowledges it without looking up. The woman on my left is silent. "How did they die?" I ask, always unsure of what to do when faced with these truths, these vulnerable lives laid out before me.

"They were sick," she said, "hot and vomiting and diarrhea. From when they were sick to when they died was six hours," she said, looking up to see my face. Before she knew what to do, they were gone. They were still.

We are quiet, the women inscrutable. I am trying to reconcile the truth of this story, this suffering, sitting next to me in a plastic chair; a horrible, asinine worksheet in front of her; and the tweet I had barely glanced at a few days ago. After a few moments, we keep reading, keep penciling in our answers, carefully scrubbing away the mistakes. When it is time to go home, I want to hug her, clasp her arm, and say that I am both sorry about her daughters and thankful I met her. But I don't. Instead, I say, like I always do, "See you next Wednesday."

"Inshallah," she says, and I wonder if she means it.

I am not poor. I drink lattes during droughts, eat hamburgers during famines. I profit off the world I was born into, an economic system that crushes and oppresses. The problem was that I was born at the top, and so all of those troubles at the bottom used to seem so hazy to me. This is the real problem of being rich and happy and healthy and popular: it becomes easy, oh so easy, to forget about the rest.

At first, these harsh words of Jesus—woe to you who are rich, woe to you who are well fed now—they used to unnerve me; they were a mirror I did not have the stomach to look into. Look away, hurry on to the other scriptures, get to the redemption, the mission you are chosen to do, try your hardest to be good, and earn the love of Jesus in the end.

But now I am drawn like a moth to the flame of hurt dripping from nearly every page of the Bible, the great sadness that shocks me out of my stupor. I am swallowed whole. I see how the anger of the Lord burns, in those days and these, hot and quick and clean. I am glad God is angry about the things that really matter: injustice, inequality, any human on this earth being treated as less than what they are, which is a child of the most bountiful God. I am glad he is angry because it shows me how much he loves.

I am poor, in that I do not know how to love people just as they are. I am poor, in that I do not know how to love myself if I am not actively giving something. I am poor, in that I do not know if I have the strength to see the kingdom of God as it was meant to be played out. I have a poverty of relationships, in that the more I try to forget about the evils of our age and my own responsibility to them, the more my heart is revealed for what it is. In reality, I am impoverished. I am starving. I am weeping. I am oppressed by a world that runs in opposition to the dreams of God.

And only when I recognize how poor I really am do I start to understand that I am right where I need to be.

On Motherhood, On Death

When there was finally a boy, and we got married, I officially had something to offer. Now all the Somali Bantu women in our apartment complex wanted to talk to me, our conversations always revolving around babies and the pain of childbirth (a universal subject, if there ever was one). They loved telling me about every single birth (and these women had many, many children), of every ache and pain, and even of the babies that didn't make it. I nodded, trying to appear proper parts interested and sorrowful, all the while feeling a little faint.

A couple of years into marriage and one month off the pill ("Oh, let's just make some 'space' for God to give us a baby," I recall blithely telling my husband), I was pregnant, trying to understand a body that didn't really seem cut out for this kind of thing. My own mother, who had borne four children and was an exceptionally fit and beautiful woman, told me stories of how much she enjoyed (and glowed during) her own pregnancies. I was miserable and heavy and tinged with gray, finishing up my grad school and working terrible retail jobs to pay the bills. And then I was in the home stretch, only two more months to go.

I threw myself into life at the complex to escape my own weary body. We did basketball camps, summer reading programs at the library, and weekly visits to the pool. I made plans to take several of my refugee neighbors to the beach, coordinating van rentals and volunteer drivers for all the aunties and uncles and cousins who wanted to come too. At the last minute, the women sat me down and told me they wouldn't be going anywhere with me. For the past few weeks, whenever I would come to visit in their apartments, they would ply me with slices of oranges and scalding cups of tea, retreating to huddle together and have hushed and urgent conversations, always pointing and tsking about the size of my ankles. This time, we were sitting in the park and watching the children play when they patted my legs. "No beach," they told me, waving their hands at my belly. "We can go next year, with you and the baby." I was mystified by how they could barely look at me. I pleaded and begged and swore I felt just great, but they continued to pat me and lie through their teeth: next year, next summer, if you are even here at all.

When I woke up so swollen I could barely open my eyes, I thought it strange. On the way to doing other important errands, I stopped in at the local hospital to get my blood pressure checked. The nurses frowned, ever so slightly, and the air changed. The afternoon stretched on, a forced sort of cheerfulness underlying all the tests and paperwork and chart-checking. A strange doctor came into the room to chat, and I couldn't understand what he wanted from me. He talked about my liver failure, of the blood pumping and exhausting my heart, of platelets being destroyed and the imminent refusal to clot. I thought, *He must be talking to someone else. I'm young, healthy, and prepared for and committed to a natural birth.* I barely heard him say that the only cure for me was delivery. That I would not be leaving the hospital until I had the baby.

That moment, in the room, felt so familiar. I had watched a lot of ER dramas in my day, so I understood the layout of gray-blue tiles and fluorescent lights, the beeping machinery and murmured voices. What I didn't expect to feel was the aching sense of loneliness inherent in surgery, of being prepped by faceless strangers for the unknown. Shoulders slumping, a giant needle stuck in my back, I thought for the first time that I really might be dying. I felt too sick to imagine the ending of this particular scenario, much too tired to grieve my carefully laid plans. My blood was pounding too hard, too fast, my temples throbbing. I couldn't pray, but it was strangely easy to imagine Jesus sitting next to me, not saying anything at all. And then, like I suppose it always happens, all I could think were the mundane thoughts: *Our apartment is a mess. I'm supposed to be at work tomorrow.* And, *Oh my gosh, we don't even own a crib.*

Our apartment was warm on the fourth floor, and we lived on the couch with the baby nestled alternately on our chests, a style the nurses called "kangaroo care." The baby was fine, an inscrutable little gnome, four pounds, perfect. We spent two weeks in that small hospital, ours the only baby in the makeshift NICU. As I was too ill to do anything for those two weeks, I sat and watched my husband, surrounded by adoring nurses, turn into an extremely capable father. Once home, friends came out of the woodwork to bring us food, impossibly tiny clothes, hand sanitizer. Everyone talked quietly in our apartment. For our non-refugee friends, we were some of the first people they knew to have a baby. We were also the first to have a brush with mortality, to be a kink in the narrative of happy hippie mommas that we all wanted to live. As people cooed over the baby, I liked to nonchalantly announce that we had both almost died. There were slightly shocked faces, profuse exclamations of gratitude. But I could see in their eyes that nobody really believed me because I didn't believe it myself. I was too young, too healthy, this could not possibly be true.

Some of the Somali Bantu people in our apartment complex told me they waited forty days to name their babies. For forty days after the baby is born, a mother would stay in her apartment, and people came to visit, cook food, and clean. She would just sit with her baby, exhausted, presumably enjoying the attention. It always perplexed me that someone would wait forty days to have a naming ceremony. And then I realized, for all the women I knew in this community, they all had several dead babies each. The forty-day ceremony was a way of preparing for the possibility of tragedy, the likelihood of which was great in the refugee camps.

After several months, some of our Somali Bantu friends finally came to visit. They didn't want to hold the baby; they felt no need to comment on how cute she was, how she had no hair. They just looked at her, asked me a few questions about the birth. There was a soberness to our interactions and a sense of calm without the riot of pleasantries all Americans are supposed to produce at the sight of a baby. I was hurt by their inattention, but tried not to show it. I asked for advice on colic, feeding, and sleeping, sure that these original attachment mothers would have some advice for me. They didn't. They would look into the baby's wizened little face, listen as she cried. "It is good for you to stay home," they told me, and then they left.

I wondered at how seldom they came to see me, how they had so few words to share. Maybe they didn't know what to do with me or the baby; premature births as a general rule do not survive refugee life. I learned later that the condition I had is thought to be a major factor in the mortality rates of women in majority nations. If I hadn't been here, if I had been there, I and the baby would be gone.

We made it through the first year and were almost done with the second. We survived breast-feeding complications, formula, colic, developmental delays, and tests. Everything meandered into normalcy, that tiny baby could now run and shriek and declare emphatically what it is she needs right this very second. I could finally breathe. I could finally start to live with one eye on the future. But I had been unprepared for how the women still press into me, asking me when I am going to have another.

I am at the pool with my toddler and a friend. I am wearing a sensible one-piece suit, and my friend Maryan was in several layers of pants, dresses, shawls, and head scarves. Maryan still manages to look incredibly beautiful, her face open and glowing and always smiling. It is an unfairness I have to get over. Maryan loves to gossip and give advice (especially if it is not asked for), and at the pool she starts right in: she informs me that my husband will leave me and add another wife if I don't have another child soon. I stare her down and say no, that isn't going to happen. I tell her I don't think I can, physically or psychologically, have any more babies. The risk is too great, the memories too near.

She shakes her head and looks very disapproving. Unasked, she gives me tips on getting pregnant: suck on lemons, pray to meet the baby in a dream. Maryan is really preaching to herself. Her one child is nearly four, and the community pressure for more offspring is enormous. Her story has several more complicated layers, as Maryan was one of the few girls in her community to choose birth control so she could finish high school. I don't know if the doctors here don't want to help her, or if it simply is a lack of communication; whatever the case, she has been trying for over two years now to get pregnant again, with no results. But still, she is defiant, fiercely optimistic that she will soon be pregnant.

Lord, I want to believe. I want to have faith enough to bring more babies into this already-sadness-soaked world. I listen to Maryan talk, and I admire her clearheadedness regarding the entire life-giving endeavor. She knows that having babies and raising them to adulthood requires enormous sacrifices, both psychological and physical (things I would prefer not to dwell on, truth be told). At the same time, there resides in her and other women from traumatic backgrounds a flintiness borne out of too many tragedies and too many deaths. I can see it in the way they looked at my baby, so tiny and helpless, and in the way they looked at me. Motherhood, that great universal experience, has only driven me farther away from these women. There is no solidarity here, only an uneasy glance into the inequality of the world.

At the pool, I feel so guilty, and I listen to Maryan. Finally, to appease her, I lie through my teeth and say maybe next summer, we will both have more babies. She smiles and nods, happy that I have come around. Maybe next summer, if we are even here at all.

Consider the Turtles

When I was four months pregnant with my second baby, I had a dream in which I gave birth to a turtle. As it often happens in dreams, this did not upset me—it merely came as a surprise. An old friend from high school was there, and as he cradled the turtle in his arms he told me something about their nature. "The thing about turtles," he said, looking solemnly and reverently at the creature, "is that when your heart breaks, their heart breaks." I woke up with that sentence reverberating in my head. I had only just begun to discover this truth, that babies and mothers are so intricately connected that our ability to hurt and wound and bind up one another was far deeper than I had ever realized.

After the trauma of the birth of my first baby, I had told my husband we would be adopting. No more biological babies. The desire had always been there in my heart, a little worm eating away at the traditional family narratives: a little squishy brown baby, a tiny girl from China, someone in desperate need of my loving arms, a win-win situation, the smiling diverse-looking Christmas cards. I told my husband we would be adopting through foster care.

A few years after my daughter was born, we wanted to start pursuing our dream of growing our family. We start the process of foster care by going to a two-hour informational meeting. Those of us in the room all say why we are there. I sense deep anguish underneath every single introduction, the tough and the vulnerable. I see how every single one of us is damaged, and we are here to learn about the damaged children in our community.

The woman doing the training tells us horror story after horror story, sometimes about foster families, but usually about the birth parents. Children whose teeth rot out due to neglect, who must have them all pulled. We learn that kids who are neglected tend to be good sleepers. They have lost the idea that someone might be there to take care of them in the middle of the night. Good sleepers, good soldiers—so many children in our world who learn so young that they are all alone in the world, that there is no one coming to check on them when they cry, so it is best to hold back the tears after all.

I hear other stories from other trainings. A woman stands at the front of the room, holding a glass half-filled with vodka. At the beginning of the training, she cracks an egg into the glass; by the end of the evening, she shows it to the room full of prospective foster parents, and the egg white has gone from translucent to opaque. This, she tells prospective foster parents, the ones full of mixed motivations and hopes and desires, this is what happens to a baby's brain when the mother drinks alcohol. And then she tells them the truth about our state: nearly 75 percent of the children in foster care have some degree of fetal alcohol syndrome, with all of the accompanying behavior and mental health issues—soft-boiled, neglected, abused, forgotten, unseen, in utero, alone out in the world. The breaking of hearts, so intricately connected, starts far before we ever see it.

I once went to the beach and discovered the wreckage from a tsunami half the world away littering the sand. Every few yards, tangled in seaweed and debris, were dead birds as far up the Oregon coast as the eye could see. They were beautiful little birds for which I had no frame of reference: white-breasted, black-feathered, little blue feet pointed up to the sky. The birds made me question a world where the sun could shine so freely on all that wreckage and a God who thought nothing of beautiful blue little feet being left to rot in the sand. It was just one tiny scene of despair that I walked through that day, a picture of our world in miniature. I had come to the beach to find God; what if, perhaps, this is what God was?

There are children with bruises running up and down their legs, babies who have given up on tears, children huddled in corners while they try not to watch what is happening in front of them. There are babies born of incest and rape and children who aren't given the correct medicine. There are so many little souls in our world both forgotten and abused, tiny broken hearts at the peripheries of our world. I want to save them all, scoop them up in my arms. I want it to stop. I have crazy thoughts. I am mad at a God who lets them be born when he knows what is to come. I am angry that I am surprised and shocked and saddened by these stories when to so many they are "just life." I will save them all, I decide, I will do it with my own magnanimous, unbroken heart.

At the same time we attend the foster care trainings, fill out the paperwork, and get our fingerprints done, we start to talk more with our neighbors. We had moved into a low-income apartment complex where the majority of people were not refugees and immigrants, but people who had grown up in generational poverty in America. It was such a distinct and foreign culture to me that it seemed we had been born in other countries. In this apartment complex, the friendships were slow to bloom, where we looked different from everyone else and where there was a delicate dance of loneliness and isolation and prejudice to constantly be aware of. My oldest daughter was two, and she and her wild blond hair roamed the hallways with abandon. She did not seem to notice the shouting fights or the tight silences or the cops rushing in. If someone offered her a bit of friendliness, she latched on with all of her strength, beaming and waving, her affection bought with a single piece of hard candy and a kind word. I tried to do the same, but there was more shame in my heart—shame that my reality was so different from those of my neighbors, shame that I was only just now starting to realize that there are two Americas that operate side by side.

We did not talk about our decision to adopt through foster care, but our neighbors occasionally mentioned "The System," as they called it. They talked about how they had been placed in foster care when they were children: they talked of sitting in cars while the white foster parents went inside to church, of being constantly reminded of their otherness, their impermanence. They had hazy memories of mothers walking up the driveway for a visit before disappearing into thin air. Some talked in short snippets about their own children being taken away: a sentence about them being adopted out, of trying to send presents at Christmas only to be told your daughter never was allowed to open them, kids who were taken and whose lives went on without you, children who ended up dying too young of liver failure, or who live on the streets, or who came back and found you all these years later, children who are in a new rehab program, children who you now celebrate precarious holidays with.

I could stand outside our apartment building, low and squat and ugly with brick and chain-link fences, and I could pick out the apartments of people I knew, people who had begun to know me and my little family in the small ways that neighbors do: I could see the touch of broken hearts on all of them. My own toddler clutched in my arms, my own heart aching for more babies, I started to realize that so many of the people we now knew either had been in the system at one point in their lives, or their kids had been taken from them. I heard it whispered and said in a myriad of ways, my neighbors taking stock of the situation around them: foster care is white people taking our children. The thorn of this stuck in my side and would not leave, burrowing deeper and deeper even as we continued our march of meetings and caseworkers and late nights spent googling behavioral issues. I began to see my neighbors and their willingness to be honest with me as one of the greatest gifts of vulnerability I had ever received. I began to see the picture that is so often cropped out of the narratives that we tell ourselves as we grow our families: that the ties are never neatly cut off, that we are all so much more connected than we would like to believe, that we are all breaking each other's hearts all the time, and that there is no way to stop it, no way to erase it. I thought I could change it, that I could save one little heart that I could fold into my own. But the hearts around me had already splintered, and I was beginning to get a sense that God was not interested in my little family, in my Christmas postcard. I was beginning to get a sense that, to God, we are all his children, even when we have children of our own and do terrible things to them. We are the ultimate vessels of sorrow. We are breaking God's heart all the time. And like a glutton for punishment, he never stops calling for us. He never stops bringing his children into the world.

For far too long the only narrative I believed was the one where I came in and cleaned it all up and took it upon my own two shoulders—where I was the infinite in the wide, gaping ocean of sorrow. The only story I was told was the one in which people like myself—good hearts, clear eyes, secure bank accounts, and family structures—would swoop in like a helicopter to save those little turtles who had been shipwrecked by life. We viewed them as autonomous, gorgeous victims; we carved spaces just big enough for them in our hearts and in our families.

I never once was told about all the connections these children have to the world around them, how their mothers and fathers are broken and bruised as well and how they were most likely left to wash up on the shores of life. I was never once urged to connect with them, to burrow myself into the long chains of systemic injustice that was the undercurrent in our world of the haves and have-nots. I was never once told to love the mothers and fathers of our most damaged children, to think about the myriad of difficult and tangled and decades-long relationships it would take to be a small part of keeping families together. I know it is too hard, too uncertain, too messy to view everyone, no matter how old and how broken, as a child of God, not just the tiny fragile ones.

But my neighbors taught me this, and I could not forget it. My husband and I told our caseworker we were ending the process, that we wouldn't be able to foster any children in the near future. We looked for other avenues, ways to support families before they splinter, ways to pursue kinship and wholeness instead of just our own picture-perfect future. We were afraid, but we decided to try for another baby, knowing full well the risks we were entering into. All the ways of bringing babies into our family were fraught with sorrow, and all of them contained a lack of control that made me wild with fear. But to choose to bring life into the world and to choose to seek ways to keep lives together—we couldn't help but feel like we were giving the finger to the darkness that seemed to surround us. We couldn't help but feel a tiny bit brave, even as we were swallowed up in sadness.

Because I was starting to believe it: his eye is on the sparrow; his eye is on the blue-footed birds littering the coast. His eye is on the children, cast aside to abuse and neglect. His eye is on the parents, so intricately connected by biology and spirit. His eye is on me, on the baby inside, on the people I live and move and love with. And all of us are slowly making our way to God, our hearts already broken by the time we arrive, searching for the only one who truly sees it all, the one who will never look away, the one who counts each and every fallen sparrow, each and every broken turtle.

Oh, to Be of Use

I always thought I was a shy and quiet child, but the reality is that I was slightly anxious, greatly unforgiving, and desperate to please God. My sisters remind me that my nickname in childhood was "the holy spirit." I declared to my parents at age six that I wanted to be a part-time missionary / full-time sarcastic comedienne to Madagascar. When they laughed, I was hurt. I was deadly serious, until I was twelve and found out that Madagascar had been colonized and populated by rich Westerners, at which point I lost interest.

But that drive to be right and to live right stayed in my guts even as it shifted forms a bit. I just want to be of use. I just want to help. I just want to make things right. It is why I jumped in feet-first to the tangle of refugee families living on the edges of my city, and it is why, for a while, it made me feel so damn good. All along, even as a small child, I was aware of the inequalities of the world, and I was at a loss as to how I could make them better. Like a constant drumbeat, an awareness of injustice and inequality grew louder and louder in my ears as my life went on and the deficits between my reality and the reality of so many of my friends and neighbors became more apparent. I still wanted to save everybody, but I also wanted to redeem myself. I was ashamed of my privilege and position, but I didn't quite know that yet. I was just trying to bring about a more equitable kingdom, with my own two hands. I was just trying to do a job that was never meant for me. I was trying to convict us all. I was trying to be the Holy Spirit.

But instead, the Spirit met me.

Once, for a year or two, my husband and I were caretakers for the low-income apartment complex where we lived. This was an exercise in futility if there ever was one. The carpets would always be stained, no matter how much we vacuumed. The doors would always be streaked by years of scratches and abuse, no matter how much we scrubbed. The walls of one floor would stay clean for a day, and then the dust and webs of life would take over, all of our work for naught.

The first month we were there, we were excited at the prospect of cleaning up the place. We bought sponges, soap, towels, and those strange little white squares simply known as "Magic Erasers." We enthusiastically started attacking the doors to the stairways on each of the three floors, on both ends of the complex. Some of the stains came off, revealing dull blue doors that had seen many a washing, with deep scratches revealing the rust and the metal underneath. As we sweated and scrubbed, smiling brightly at our new neighbors, trying to convey appropriate amounts of Jesus-ness and good cheer, one of our new neighbors stopped us. "You both sure do like to clean, don't you?" he asked. He didn't say it in a nice way, either. He leaned on the door frame and squinted at us, and I could see it all in his face. There was no way to win, in this situation. We were young, we were white, and we had moved in and taken the job of caretakers. If we did a poor job cleaning, we would know it. But if we tried too hard to clean—insinuating that everyone before we came to "help" lived in squalor—we would be told off as well. We stood there, buckets dripping and full of grimy water. We stood there, and could think of no proper response to our neighbor. And this is when we started to think about the myriad of facets there are to gentrification, how there are no easy answers or solutions, only a thousand ways to make mistakes, a thousand ways to pick yourself up and keep trying.

As I traveled down the path of the stateless wanderers, finding kinship with refugees and immigrants, I stumbled into another world as well: the world of people who have grown up in generational poverty in America. I saw it as we worked in communities that were mired in it, as well as when we explored the foster care system and learned about how it had affected those living around us—children, but also mothers and fathers and grandparents. A few years ago, my small family planted ourselves in the most diverse neighborhood in all of America, soaking up the differences while striving for commonalities. Our new neighborhood had a rich history of African-American and Native-American populations, and it was also a space where wave after wave of immigrants and refugees crashed on the shores a decade or two after the wars in their own countries caused them to seek asylum.

In our new apartment, our new neighborhood, we were thrilled as only white people can be, gentrifiers in every sense of the word, experiencing the benefits of diverse culture and cheap rent while having no knowledge or experience in the systemic injustices that governed the lives of many of our new neighbors. While we had lived in low-income housing before, we still managed to view it all as a bit of a lark, an "experiment" in downward mobility.

But things change when you start to allow the experience of your neighbors to shape you, instead of the other way around. We started to see how things that were easy for us were fraught with complications for many of our neighbors: obtaining fair housing, experiencing limited interactions with the police (who were always respectful to us), having easy access to fair-wage jobs, and enjoying a much lower propensity to be caught (and charged) for minor civil infractions. For a while, we were unable to comprehend what we were seeing and experiencing as bystanders in a divided America. Eventually, the weight of the truth started to settle on our shoulders, calling a grief that we never knew was in us, a form of lament that threatened to overwhelm us if we let it.

And one day, it did.

The day our neighbor came over and watched my husband and I pour our spirits out was a day that forever changed me. Grieved and imprisoned by our own wounds, the persistent lies we were fed and nurtured, the histories that we swallowed whole, the sins as old as time, we pleaded with him to help us understand. There was a black boy who died, and the person who killed him was let go. Our neighbor stayed for coffee and let us talk, and then he said: "You have the luxury of being surprised. Nobody else around here is." In his astounding kindness, my neighbor stayed and talked with us, patient and sorrowful, his weariness more harrowing to my soul than I could begin to understand. That one sentence—You have the luxury of being surprised—will stay with me the rest of my life, a testament to a privilege I no longer want.

At one point in my life, desperate for some solidarity, I e-mailed a much-admired revolutionary author, one who had inspired me with his stories of redemption and reconciliation. "Help," I wrote. "I moved in somewhere to love my neighbors, and one of them is spiraling back into an addiction and taking several other people down with him. He is loud, violent, and I am afraid. What do I do?" The author gently advised me to invite this man over to my house for dinner, that soup and conversation could change the world. I read his e-mail, so full of hope and grace, and I closed my computer, despondent at my own lack of saintliness. I did not invite my neighbor over for dinner. I was chained by my own fear, ignorance, and a genuine lack of experience with situations so far outside of my norm. I, like everyone else on my floor, remained inside the day the police came to take my spiraling neighbor away, guns drawn. "Failure, failure, failure," the song started singing inside of me. Why can't my life be one big potluck, full of the tattooed and dreadlocked kind Christian hippies and the grateful sober? Why is the reality so much more dark and small and full of uncertainty, every little thing I do a mistake of some kind, some gesture of privilege or of a savior complex or gentrification?

"Living life with intentionality," we blithely said, but what we meant was that we were excited to be slumming it for Jesus, and we assumed we would make everything better based on our presence alone. But it didn't take long for us to come to a point where we didn't know which way was up, where the blessings that Jesus talked about started to feel more like a curse, and where our neighbors became a dull knife scraping at all of our sins of pride and selfishness and fear.

Robert Coles was a genius of a man, a psychologist and writer and lover of great literature. He was also a Christian, and he was intensely interested in hearing and amplifying the unheard voices of his time. Coles was the one tasked with interviewing and counseling Ruby Bridges, the first little black girl to integrate in New Orleans in 1960. Coles went on to interview many, many more children, most of them from marginalized communities; he would ask them to color pictures and talk to him about whatever they wanted. The insights he received, as well as the resilience that he witnessed, were astounding. Once, a little black girl from Mississippi drew a picture of herself. She explained to Coles, "That's me, and the Lord made me. When I grow up my momma says I may not like how He made me, but I must always remember that He did it, and it's His idea. So when I draw the Lord, He'll be a real big man. He has to be, to explain the way things are."

I am on the other side of that picture: I come from the places of power and privilege, but I still need the Lord to explain some things to me. My choice of neighborhoods is just the start of me trying to scale the large mountains of alienation that are inside of me. I feel like I see the wounds of Christ bright red in front of me, but I am still not able to feel them.

That people prefer themselves and all others like them is no surprise to any of us, but I am consistently taken aback at how often we refuse to acknowledge that our systems might have the same kind of problem. Being the minority where I work and live and play has opened my eyes to the way the systems (political and religious) are intrinsically *for me*. This never bothered me until I realized what the converse of that equation is: those systems are actively against others.

That realization alone is enough to stop me. The words "sin" and "repentance" and "judgment" are infused with new meaning. True repentance, I was always taught, involves turning away from myself and turning toward God. Now, it has meant turning toward the ones who are being shut out.

It is this: moving in, listening, reading books. Putting myself in a position to be wrong, to be silent, to be chastised, to be extended forgiveness, to withhold judgment, to invite understanding. I thought the cost would be steep, but it has turned out to be the opposite. *You have the luxury of being surprised.* And surprised I have been—how I have seen and heard and felt the Spirit convict me, how I am starting to understand how unwell I have been all this time. And the flip side is this: as it turns out, I am exactly the kind of person Jesus came for. He can only heal us once we figure out that we can't be of any use at all. He can do it, because he's a real big man. He has to be, just to explain the way things are.

The Rule of Life

Dorothy Day's Rule of Life:

See the face of Christ in the poor.
And: journal every day.

The first time I saw the buildings, they buzzed. In my evangelical fever I didn't know if it was electricity, demons, or just the sounds of thousands of souls put in close proximity together. This is where I want to live, I told my husband, shading my eyes to see the tops of the high-rises. This low-income housing in the sky, one of the last few remaining, a testament to the enduring imagination of how to contain the poor in America. In the end, we didn't move in, cautioned by well-meaning friends. You would burn out like a beautiful flame, they told me, and I didn't know how to tell them that this was exactly what I wanted.

I started volunteering at the English school there, large and chaotic classes held in the community center. The walls inside were painted a claustrophobic electric orange; I imagined the hallways caving in on me. In the beginning, it was fascinating, and a little terrifying; it was easy to believe I was a little flame for God, walking through the underpasses of the world. The students rolled into class whenever they felt like it; they shouted and laughed at one another; they showed up even as their lives

D. L. MAYFIELD

fell apart, phone call by phone call. They came even though they had never been in a class before.

There were so many of them. They were learning how to arrive, sit down, store their papers in a binder, wait their turn to speak, look from left to right on the page, understand that the scratches on the board corresponded to sounds, words, and concepts. The rooms filled up, students spilling into the hallways. I told the bosses to hire me, that they needed someone to teach the ABCs to all those who had never learned the skills before, the learning curves steep and debilitating. They said sure, you can start next week. The fire within me flamed up, fed by the intoxicating feeling of being needed.

We are going over the alphabet, again, just as we have for months now. A few students know the names of the letters, can match the sounds, and pick out a few token sight words. But the majority are lost; I am dragging them with me on a trail littered with reminders of how the world has not done right by them. These women, denied access to education due to their gender, their poverty, their birthplace being choked with war and the all-consuming quest for survival—I just need them to write their own names. Or at least recognize which letter of the alphabet they start with.

After several months, there are still few who can do this. But the ones who catch on, building tenuous connections, little spiderwebs of understanding, they do not escape our collective notice. "Samia," I say, noticing one woman's careful and neat handwriting. "Did you ever go to school in Ethiopia?" She looks at me, surprised. "No," she says. I thought for a moment she would say yes—she is my miracle, the student I cling to, the only one who makes me feel like I might be doing something of value. I will have to move her up a level soon, but I don't want to let her go.

Before I know what is happening, everyone is trying to tell me, in their very limited conversational English, why they didn't go to school. They communicate in words, not sentences, with hand motions, pantomimes, and exaggerated faces. I do it, too. I am a children's TV show host around them, utterly abandoned to my attempts at communication. I will play the fool, if only to see them smile.

One woman shows me how her husband held her hands down, her wrists crossed in front of her. Another tells me that her father said no, no, no school for you. Another scorns the others, pities them, and tells me, oh no, my family was very good. My family was not like this. "In my family," she said, "two girls got to go to school. But one girl needed to stay and watch the goats." She does not need to say it: it just happened that she was that girl.

At first I am pleased, thinking we are creating a safe space here for this kind of dialogue. Mining the depths of poverty, oppression, war, disruption. They tell me the stories that got them to this point today, staring at senseless pieces of paper, but they do not feel better. Their growing awareness of the difficulties they have with memory retention, the way their life is not the same as others—it is not a sweet pill to swallow. Women are looking down, their faces settling into grave and quiet lines that they rarely let me see. Up front, limp and helpless, stupid with my English-only words, I realize that this is not a safe space at all. It is a place where our deficits are shoved in our faces, time and time again.

Johara picks up her pencil and leans back in her chair. "But we are here," she says loudly, hitting her binder for emphasis. "We are here! Now! English class!" And so they go back to squinting at a page of ABCs, the same one they have looked at four times a week for the past eight weeks, the words still appearing as minnows swimming across a lily-white pond. Point to the letter that your name starts with, I tell Amina and Habiba and Maryan and Fadumo. They stare at me, then down at the paper. They know these specific scratches mean so much to me, the teacher. They know, but they do not understand, why that nice girl so badly needs them to do this.

You are not supposed to have favorites, but Amina is mine. She wears the same clothes four days a week, her hijab always clean. Her spoken English is the best in the class; she is my guide and translator. Everything is *Alhamdulillah,* all praise be to God. You can't keep her down. She will not let you.

Amina cannot remember what letters make what sounds. She guesses, wildly and incorrectly. She laughs, crinkling her nose. When she is very lost in class, she starts singing Somali wedding songs. Her voice is high-pitched and lonely and beautiful. When she does not smile, my stomach falls into a pit, dark and wide as her eyes. She is too young to have ten children, but she does. She is too lovely to have a sick husband, a country that will never hold a place for her again, a job cleaning hotel rooms near the airport, a mind that refuses to remember printed words.

Sofia, the veteran of the group—the sharp-tongued grandmother, enrobed in several thick woolen sweaters—makes a comment about Amina in class. She says it in English, so I will hear it. We are all reading from the board, and Amina is guessing, laughing after each quiet correction. Sofia says, "Amina is crazy." She makes the universal motions associated with this: a pointer finger aimed at her temple, going around in slow circles. Sofia, encouraged by the chuckles of a few other students, says it again. "Amina is crazy. No English. No reading."

"No," I tell Sofia, trying to be firm without being sharp, conscious of the gap in age and culture and life experience. "No, we don't say that. Amina is not crazy. Amina is number one." Sofia turns to the side and laughs with her companion. Amina is not smiling, and she is older and more tired than I can possibly imagine. But then she does, the familiar crinkles appearing. She too points her finger at her temple, laughing at herself. "Crazy, crazy," she says, mining it all for a laugh. It is becoming increasingly clear to us all that she might never learn to read or write. "Amina is crazy," she says again. She claps her hands together and raises them to the sky. Alhamdulillah.

Rukia does not walk in late. She arrives as a hurricane, picking up her skirts with one hand, her backpack falling across a shoulder, shouting jokes to somebody across the other side of the room. "The train, teacher," she tells me. "Late." "Okay, okay, Rukia. Can you find this paper for me?" She takes the crumpled pages out of her backpack, scatters them around the table. They are upside down. She doesn't notice. She shakes my hand, and her fingers are freezing. "Where are your gloves?" I ask, and she shakes her head no. It is the coldest winter we have had in thirty years. In thirty minutes, Rukia holds up her hands to me again. They still feel cold, but she is telling me that they are hurting. I am relieved. Pain is good. Pain means you are alive. The next day I bring gloves for her, and she wears them on the train ride home. But the next time I see her, her hands are bare and cracked. The weather is below freezing. The wind makes me hate the world. I am frustrated, disappointed, sighing as I shake her hand good morning. Teacher, teacher, she laughs as she comes in late again. She is the one who likes to tell the other students to be quiet, unaware that she is the loudest, most disruptive student of them all. She is the one who has a very sick child in the hospital, his ventricles filled with fluid. She is the one who can now spell her own name, slow and scattered. She is the one whose fingers ache, all winter long. She is the one who moved here for a better life. She is the one who is living in a shelter downtown. She is the one who gave the gloves to her daughter.

"Turn phones off," I repeat, pantomiming the process. Yes, yes, teacher, they say, but they do not turn them off. The phones ring throughout class, our one true constant. They have no numeracy skills, no way of recognizing who is calling. It could be a family member from Africa, asking for a money order. It could be a caseworker, calling with a housing appointment. It could be the government, canceling medical benefits or food stamps. It could be a telemarketer, a wrong number. It could be anyone at all.

Okay, okay, students. They answer the phones, but they must step into the hallway. They clutch the black compact flipphones to their hijabs, they whisper and shout. I go on with class, pretending I cannot hear.

Nadifa answers the phone in class. She turns away, twisting her torso in her seat, thinking maybe I will not notice. But I do, and tell her to please get up and walk to the hallway. She ignores me, concentrating on the call. Suddenly she hangs up, and she is crying. She is standing up suddenly, scraping the chair against the floor. She is shuffling the papers, shoving her worksheets into a bag filled with her refugee identification cards and I-9 forms, the scrap of paper with her address on it, the phone number for her caseworker. Everything she has, in one little bag.

Seeing Nadifa cry unnerves me. I am flustered, asking, "What's wrong? What happened?" Everyone is talking in Somali, and I am lost, the forgotten, the background player in an all-encompassing drama. Nadifa is a rock of a woman, slow to smile and slow to speak, getting more pregnant by the day. She is one of the best students in the class, but she is one of the few who does not call me sister, does not engulf me in hugs on the way out. Amina and Sofia speak for her, as she packs up her things. The day care called, they say. Her son is having a seizure. She needs to go meet them at the hospital.

"Oh, Nadifa," I say, aware of how few words I have for this. "I am so sorry." She nods at me, sniffing loudly. In the past few months, I have heard many sad stories, but I have never seen a single tear. I try and pat her arm. She shakes her head, says something else in Somali. Amina translates: "She says she forgot to give him his medicine today." For once, the class is mostly silent. We are all watching Nadifa walk out the door. She says, "My husband just left me and I have five children. What can I do?"

I am left up front, a lesson plan clutched in my hand. I am mute and my mind is an empty page until I hear the students mutter Alhamdulillah, ready to get back to class. All praise to God. No use complaining. Everything is the will of God.

I find myself shouting like a heretic: "No, no, NO Alhamdulillah!" Everything is not okay. The students are staring at me, entranced by the composure melting away, watching as my professional boundaries are splintered. This is not God's dream for the world, I am saying in English, knowing it will sound like nonsense. Now I am crying, both bitter and embarrassed at my co-opted grief.

Oh, teacher. The students look at me with concern. They stand up and hug me, and I am crying because I am angry. Don't feel bad for me, I want to tell them. Instead I say, with more fierceness than I intended: "Pray, *salat,* for Nadifa." They are still looking at me. Now, I say, louder: "Pray for Nadifa's *wiil,* Nadifa's son." They look at one another, and look at my tear-stained face. "Okay, teacher," they say, and they lift their palms up and start to recite the words they know by heart.

One day I wear a scarf to work, one I bartered for at the nearby Somali mall. It is gauzy white with beautiful blue and pink swirls. The students compliment me, excited over every little commonality I try for. The few Somali or Arabic words I speak, my avowed hatred for dogs, the fact that my daughter's name sounds similar to one of their own. "Teacher, teacher," they say, when we talk about prayer and wanting to follow God. "You are *this* close to being a Muslim." They hold their thumbs and pointer fingers close together. "You are this close."

Ifrah gets up and is humming a song to herself. She shuffles up to me and starts to rearrange my scarf. Before I know what is happening, she is turning it into a head covering. Tight around my face, tucked over my head and back around again. Not a wisp of hair or ears to be seen. The students clap, their faces delighted. I laugh and thank Ifrah, but inside I am nervous at what this means.

At break, I go to the bathroom and catch a glimpse of myself in the mirror. I immediately want to cry. Not because I am offended by this signifier of difference or that I feel conflicted with my Christian missionary upbringing. The head scarf brings out the fullness in my face, as round and doughy as a pillow, dark shadows creasing under my eyes. I want to cry because I am vain. I want to cry because I am so different from my students, and there is no way to pretend otherwise. I pull it off my head and go back to class. When I eventually stop wearing scarves to work, my students do not say anything.

In class, they were all talking so loudly, with an edge, that I thought they were fighting. "Please," I say. They remember I am there, and they try to explain. A man died. No, a woman died. No, a man killed his wife. They are slashing their fingers over their throats, over and over again, eager for me to understand. I don't understand. I run out of the classroom and across the courtyard to the office. I run past the primary-colored playground, surrounded on all sides by buildings tall enough that the sun will never touch down on the children. I stop several men, asking if they can come translate for me. One finally agrees, and comes with me. He is wearing a sweater vest. He tells me a Somali man who was living at the shelter committed suicide on Saturday, the day between Good Friday and Easter Sunday. Many of the students knew him and his wife. He got a letter in the mail saying he had been denied housing benefits and that, due to a previous mishap with an employer, his future wages would be garnished. The man thought he would never rent or work again; perhaps he couldn't read, and someone explained it wrongly to him. And so he hung himself.

There was no class that day. Instead I made coffee the way we all liked it: strong, thick with cream and sugar. A Somali proverb declares that when you have lived to a ripe old age, you can put as much sugar in your tea as you would like. We surely deserve the sweet to go with the bitterness of outliving so many. Someone tells me an address where Hawo, the widow, is staying, and it is around the corner from my place. I knew I couldn't help her, and she was just one of many. I am a bed of coals, numbed and gray-edged; but I know I will go visit before I even say the words aloud.

I will see it with my own eyes. Other students write down their own addresses on pieces of paper. I put them in my briefcase. Surely, there are other people who are helping them. It cannot possibly just be me. I am comforted by this thought, but there is no way to know if it is true.

At the apartment building, I follow a Somali woman up the steps. I ask her where Hawo is. She does not understand. I think about making the throat slashing gesture, but stop myself. I am here for Mohammed, the man who died, I say, and she nods her head and motions for me to follow her. We go up to the third floor, and there are shoes spilling out into the hallway. I take mine off and watch as everyone adjusts to my presence. I know no one, but I repeat the names of my students, the ones who told me about the death. Hawo, the widow, is not there. Her mother is, sitting on the floor, holding a small and delicate baby in her arms. The baby's eyes are lined with kohl. They tell me she is Hawo's child, and she was born twenty-one days ago. They bring me a straight-backed chair to sit in, and objectively I am thinking, *This is so sad*. I turn to the older children in the room, despising myself even as I do it. "Do you speak English?" I ask. "Yes," the boy answers. He looks like he is ten years old. "My dad died," he says, and he smiles. I don't want to use him to translate, but it is all I have.

Someone brings me a can of Coke, warm as blood. I drink it, and nobody says much. Later, a cousin with excellent pronunciation arrives and tells me it is all a mistake. His brother-in-law had a heart attack, he tells me. I push a crumpled bill into the hand of the grandmother, and stoop to look closer at the baby girl. She is one of the prettiest creatures I will ever see in my life.

Later, my students tell me it was all the wife's fault. They tell me the four-year-old son found the father hanging from the light fixture in the bathroom. They do not tell me it was his time to die. They do not say all praise to God. They do not tell me how unbearably hard life must be if you are willing to forfeit paradise just to escape it.

Once there was a river. And down that river came bodies—many of them. Bodies upon bodies, stacking up in the cool shallows. On the banks of the river, people panicked. They waded into the water and started grabbing all the bodies they could. Once on shore, these good-hearted people stopped everything and tried to resuscitate the cold, nearly lifeless bodies piling up. Everywhere you looked there were people, eyes searching the water, wading back in to pull out yet another lost one. Until, eventually, one of the people on the shore decided to look up. Where are all of these damned bodies coming from? he wondered. So he left his post on the edge of the river and started to hike upstream. He left behind the urgent work to find the source of the problem.

My friend once explained this parable to me. The people on the shore are the merciful, the ones performing triage in a world where the bodies are piling up faster than we can count them. And then there are the others. Those who look a bit higher. The justice-oriented, my friend says. They look at the systemic roots. They see the big picture. And for a while, they might need to leave their on-the-ground spot in order to get to the roots of the problems.

My friend gently suggested that I might be a justice person living in a place that is thick with the nearly drowned. I heard her, and the tears came to my eyes. As much as I would like to think of myself in that way, I knew better. All I wanted to do was forget about the river. But I had seen Christ there, floating in the shallows. There was no way I could leave.

I stare at my class roster in dismay. The list of names keeps getting longer and longer. The progress gets slower and slower. The chairs scrape and fill up. The buzz of our souls and our troubles is a constant presence. I am hopeless. For the rest of my life I will be asking people to be quiet every five minutes. When it snows, at the end of April, a small part of me is pleased. Maybe fewer people will come to class today, I think to myself. I am changing.

I draw little stars next to the names of the visibly pregnant women in my class. They make up almost a third of my students. They come and they sit down and they close their eyes. I see them from up by the whiteboard, and I am pierced with compassion. Let those blessed little lambs sleep. Later, when they wake up and will not stop talking, I count the days until I think they will give birth.

Ifrah comes to class. I again hint that perhaps it would be better for her to sleep instead of taking two buses four mornings a week to us. She smiles but says nothing. The other students tell me that today, in fact, is the day that the doctor said her baby would come. May 8. The day she has her sixth child. They are making jokes about the baby coming and teacher catching it. They know this will elicit a reaction from me, and I play it up. "Oh my gosh!" I say, clapping both hands to my cheeks. "Teacher will call 911!" Everybody is laughing. We do not stop for a good long while. Ifrah gets up every now and again, pacing the back of the classroom. She takes off her sandals. Her feet are swollen. I am nervous, keeping her always in my periphery.

As soon as I tell the students class is finished (see you on Monday, Inshallah) they gather around Ifrah. They are blessing her. They run their hands down her, from the top of her head down past her belly. They gather around and lift up their palms. Salat, salat. I don't know exactly what they are saying, but I know enough. I am blessing her too. My heart is aflame for her, for everyone gathered around her. I am so tired of pretending otherwise, of acting like making and understanding these tiny marks on the page are of any importance at all. I just want to touch her arm and say be blessed. I just want to see her be okay. I just want to know that there is someone watching over her, a love and a presence who is much more able than I am to see it all. I will pray, I tell my students. That the baby will be okay. That Ifrah will be okay.

Where are all these bodies coming from? She is a single mother, one of the other students tells me. I know. I know only the tiniest bit of her story. If I were a person of justice, I would send half of my students home. We would get down to the business of learning how to read, of learning how to navigate a Western, literacy-centric world. We would find stable housing. We would apply for jobs. We would talk about bedbugs and cockroaches and slumlords. We would advocate for our rights as women and citizens of the kingdom of heaven.

If I were a person of mercy, I would treat each student like a prophet, reverent and grateful. I would not be so hopeless; I would not write this all out. I would hide the beautiful flame that flares up and then hovers, nearly extinguished. It would not feel like the world is an endless river, that all I can do is sit on the shore and touch the bodies as they float on past.

I put my hand on Ifrah's shoulder and I pray for her, surrounded in the crush of the group. There is no way I can ever know how she is feeling in this exact moment. There is no way to know if this is of any use at all. So I say goodbye to her, and I bless her, and I hope that she does not come back on Monday.

On Healing

I went to a healing service not too long ago, full of anxious excitement. It was in a high school cafeteria, a new one, built in the past five years. There were flags from countries all around the world hung on the walls and two banners on either side of the stage. One showed the silhouette of a girl standing up, hands joyfully raised to the sky. Beside her stood an empty wheelchair, and in a jaunty font below it said, "Nothing is impossible with God!" To the right of the stage was a banner with a handful of good-looking young people caught in the middle of jumping for (apparent) joy. In all caps this time it read, "GOD'S IN A GOOD MOOD!"

Besides the banners, the flags from various countries, there was another staple of charismatic culture: the prayer flags. Shimmery, large, most tinged with iridescence, they are being waved all over the place, mostly by middle-aged women, but there are children too, grabbing smaller flags and running and shrieking, enjoying the time immensely. I see a few middle-aged men. They look like they are realtors, or salesmen, or somebody who owns a contracting business: gray hair, polo shirts, slight paunch. They wave the flags slowly and solemnly, making large arcs in the air, swinging down and twirling, and I am unprepared for the juxtaposition of their stature (middle-class white male) with the inherent lunacy of waving a shiny flag to music. But they are doing it, and I sit down in my bleacher seat, stunned at it all. I sit in the back like the delinquent I feel I am. But still, I am here. I don't want to miss out on anything good, anything holy, anything of God. This has been a driving force of most of my life, and it is tiring.

The auditorium is well lit. It is easy to imagine the well-to-do teenagers eating lunch, lounging in folding chairs, not paying attention in assemblies. But here, now, there was a sense of expectation that was, if not electric, then comfortably certain. From my perch on the top of the midsize bleachers, I could survey the crowd, an overwhelmingly mature bunch. There were gray heads everywhere, sensible looking women with slacks and sweaters and perms. The men looked like grandpas you would cast in a sitcom: balding, khakis, oversize earth-toned Hawaiian shirts. I watched this crowd as the music played, watched as these dignified people raised their hands and waited for the healer to come out and do his business, and I could tell they believed in it all. Again, I felt confused. Imagine if your grandpa believed in faith healers, if he pressed his slacks first and then went with his wife to a gymnasium, if he stood and raised his arms up to heaven, asking for a miracle, a sign from the sky.

There is a woman in a denim jumper with frizzy hair sitting directly in front of me, and she turns to her companions from time to time, gesturing at the air above our heads, eyes wide open and whisper-shouting, "It's here! I can see it! The glory of God is so thick in this place!" This is what I remember from my childhood, going to charismatic services with my mom. You can never tell if people are really into Jesus or if they are just insane. It's a fine line to walk, which is why most people I know nowadays just walk away.

I cannot explain what compelled me to come here, except that I am slowly becoming aware all the time, that there are things above and beyond me. As I have grown older, matured, and stretched into a faith that is constantly evolving, I cannot deny that the Bible is full of stories of punch and power, of healings and miracles, prophesies, and even tongues. The early Christians were a little circus-like, drawing crowds and keeping them, healing sick people and then speaking of a way to save the soul—to be healed in your head and your heart, to see the world as God intended it to be, to take your rightful place in it. The charismatics of my childhood might have been bat-shit crazy, but they believed in a very good God, one that knew what was going on, who was saddened by all the same things that made us sad, who was not content to sit by and let it all happen. He had power, he had heart.

Through various colleges, churches, and books, I had met another God, one full of justice, who hated sinners, who was full of wrath for the world. His primary mode of communication was logic, explaining right beliefs that would then lead to right actions. This God made sense, was comforting in a way (if you were following the rules, that is), this God was safe. He was also strangely absent in all of the traumas of our time, a busy deity who promised he would tidy all things up at the end of time. In the meanwhile, this is what our lot in life was, thanks to Adam and Eve and that pesky tree of knowledge.

But here, in this auditorium, there are believers. I see them, surrounding me, and I am made to feel small. When the prophet of the evening comes out he is just a preacher with a fancier title: homely and large and probably a grandfather, speaking in an exaggerated Southern drawl, repeating words and phrases over and over. He promises us all big things tonight, big things are in the air. "Tonight is different," he says, "tonight there will be big miracles." I feel very little emotion. He isn't terrible, and he isn't wonderful. He says this to all of us who are broken, sick, incomplete: "God doesn't want us this way; we don't have to stay this way. We just need faith."

The prophet decides to pray for us, and all three hundred or so attendants raise their hands to the sky. Before he gets to the praying part he stops, looks at the crowd and remarks: "You know, if I had been told there were going to be great miracles happening, I wouldn't be sitting in my seat." And before I understand the implications of the sentence, the entire crowd is on its feet, pushing toward the front, scraping metal folding chairs, a uniform and nonviolent mob of people seeking to get a touch from God. I hang back and watch as people line up, snaking across the auditorium, and the prophet shouts some instructions: a deacon will anoint everyone's head with a drop of holy oil, the prophet will come and lay hands for a moment. There will be several men moving along the line as well, placed to catch those who become overwhelmed with the Spirit and need to lie down. There is a certain amount of order here that I am relishing, an instruction manual for the bizarre, one that I wish I had heard more often. The charismatic events of my childhood and teen years were characterized by a sense of frenzy, of trying to get in on the good stuff before it all went away, of everyone experiencing something different (and usually, bigger and better than the previous person). I liked the orderliness of this night, the lines forming, the procedure of oil, touch, impartation; I liked watching it from the back of the bleachers.

But still I moved toward the front. The fluorescent lights overhead buzzed, and I waited for my turn, eyes closed. I was afraid: of looking ridiculous, that this was all a farce. But most of all, I was afraid that my unbelief would cause me to miss out on God, that I could stop myself from seeing and experiencing life for what it really was.

I prayed for my unbelief. I felt the drop of oil on my forehead; the prophet came close for half a second. He said something about an anointing—it was vague and quick and disappointing. And then the self-proclaimed prophet moved along the line, praying for the other souls, giving of the Spirit. I shook my head a bit, and walked back up to the bleachers. I saw an old neighbor of mine, the one who had told me about the healing service in the first place. She grabbed my arm as I was walking back to my seat. She was kind and earnest, wanting to know how I was doing. Out of nowhere, I started to cry. And like someone who believes in it all would, my neighbor prayed for me, right then and there. And that was all I needed, at that moment. I felt no holy rush, no buzzing, or shaking, or loss of equilibrium. But I felt listened to, and I felt encouraged by the faith of this woman, her lack of hesitation or normal social boundaries, the way she pressed in close with her palm cupped around my elbow in the middle of the high school auditorium.

As I walked back to my car, the one thing I couldn't forget were the people at the healing service who were there for much more desperate reasons, the people with wheelchairs, the children with severe developmental disabilities. They were there—some on their own volition, others brought by loving family members, faithful caregivers—and it is these people I wish I didn't have to see, the real reminders of the very different realities of our world. They show me that there is God's world, a heaven of redeemed souls and bodies, a place of peace and worship and wholeness in every sense. And they show me that there is this world, where people in wheelchairs line up to get a touch underneath a banner that says anything is possible.

The rub of all this is that to Jesus, both worlds are true, and they do not negate each other. This is why he talked about the kingdom so much, as this was his way of gently telling people it was not as easy as embracing one world or the other. No pessimists or optimists allowed, only kingdom people. That Jesus was so intricately aware of the broken is made obvious by the way he chose to introduce his ministry, by the people he exclusively walked among, dined with, and became fast friends with. He did not shy away or pretend or retreat to platitudes, but pointed out the lack of unbelief in nearly everyone he interacted with.

For as many as are healed, there are more that are not, and this too is the nature of the kingdom. It has not been redeemed; yet here we are in this auditorium in our leg braces and wheelchairs, with asthma and arthritis and a heart that doesn't want to listen for fear we will hear that we are to dance, to sing, to preach, to pray. And maybe this is all we are called to do, to be healed of our blindness to the things unseen, to the miracles that happen and the miracles that don't. That it turns out Jesus was saying we were all blind in this way, and he came to heal us all.

Sitting in that healing service, I didn't know what I wanted to be healed from. Now, I think I know: I wanted to be sure that God was good and that he was at work in the world, in the lives of me and all of my stateless wanderer friends. I wanted his love and justice to pour down on me like water. I wanted to live like the Spirit was real, like God had become enmeshed with all of us, like his ways were contrary to all the successes and profitable and pleasing ways of the world.

I realized that I was tired of being comfortable with sickness and death and inequality; so, too, was I tired of being overwhelmed with all of the places where it seemed that God was absent. I was tired of trying to fix all the problems on my own, of placing the burdens of the world on my own shoulders. I had reached a breaking point, where I no longer believed I could save anybody and I didn't know if God could either. I, unlike the majority of people at the service, was afraid to give up my false sense of control. I was afraid of looking foolish, of deciding to truly believe that a very good God was at work in the world.

I was nervous to live in a world that seemed inhabited by so few, to refuse to assimilate into a life either of despair or of religious platitudes.

But really, when it comes down to it, I was scared that God might ask me to wave my own freakish, shimmering flag around—to declare that he loved all of us, when everything around me seemed to contradict this statement.

4

Stabilization

The Life-Changing Magic of Couch-Sitting

The longer I knew my refugee friends, the more ignorant I became. Or at least, this is how it seemed to me. I started off so confident, so sure of my words and actions. Over time, I became immersed in their problems, falling headfirst into a crash course on how hard it is to make it on the margins of the Empire, and I ended up becoming overwhelmed, overworked, and slightly bitter. I went from feeling like an expert to a saint to finally nursing the belief that I was a complete and utter fraud and failure, and this was the best thing that ever happened to me. It's the only way I could ever start to learn to be a listener.

I recently got the chance to talk to a teacher of the Somali language, a young man who has made it his life mission to help Westerners like me understand the culture and history of the Somali people. It isn't a very fun job in a segregated, socially stratified country such as ours. This young man was poised, soft spoken, gentle, and smart. He went around my city and educated people on customs, culture, and religion. Although he was young, he longed for the old ways of his country. He loved proverbs, the wisdom of the elders, teasing out the riddles to a happy life. He stood up in front of a classroom and fielded well-meaning but ignorant and offensive questions, over and over and over again. Questions about pirates. About polygamy. About jihad. And he answered them all with a smile on his face, politeness in his eyes, short and quick and to the point.

One day I asked him a question, one that burned in my heart but embarrassed me. It exposed so much of my own ignorance and prejudice, laid bare my own wants and needs, my own interpretation of culture. I asked him why there isn't really a word or phrase in the Somali language to say thank you, at least one that is used in everyday life.

My teacher, my friend, did not need even a moment to pause. Somali people, he said, believe in the inherent dignity of every human being. If someone asks you for a cup of cold water, you will give it to them, no questions asked. You don't need to be told thank you, because when you give the cup of water you are acknowledging that this person is a human, deserving of life, deserving of this cup of cold water. Why would you need to be told thank you? If you were thirsty, the other person would do the same for you.

His words hung there in the air, making more sense to me than I could express.

Jesus said, whatever you have done to the least of these, you have done so unto me. A cup of cold water, a jacket around the shoulders. A visit to the prison or the hospital, a knock on a long-forgotten apartment door. A steaming cup of chai, made with scalded milk and too much sugar, drunk with gratitude. And no need to say thank you, that was delicious. Just accepting it for what it is, a gift given with no expectations, a testament to how we are all made in the image of God.

In my mind, I had an idea of how the poor should act: kindly, hospitable, grateful, and downtrodden. The reality, as we all know by now, was a bit more complicated. The poor are not a people group but rather a diverse, eclectic, living and breathing mass of humanity. Among my Somali Bantu friends, I was often surprised by how little food and drink they offered me when I came over. At first, I didn't mind this at all, as it gave me a chance to observe them: Jamila and her husband, Abdi, eating in front of a coffee table covered in white linen, slightly stained and askew. They ate with their hands, having no need for utensils or conversation or exclamations of pleasure. The children sat on the floor, the carpet covered with various woven mats and topped with other carpets, sharing one large communal bowl of whatever had been cooked that day. Neighbor children, all Somali Bantu themselves, would wander in and seat themselves around the bowl, helping themselves as they saw fit. The quietness of the meal always struck me; as someone to whom mealtime has always been something to find pleasure in, never to fear, this was new to me.

Years later, I would see images from the refugee camps where these children were born and raised. I would see the mothers and fathers waiting patiently to receive their bags of millet and rice, subsistence food, calories calculated to be just enough to ensure survival and nothing more, human lives counted in energy consumed and expended, with less thought to taste than most dog food in America. In the pictures I would see, the mothers would sit and pick through the rice, discarding any rocks or inedible pieces. The children, off to the side, stared at their mothers, every ounce of their attention absorbed by the food, the one and only thing that their entire lives were now based around. Getting and preparing food was a life-or-death experience in those desert camps: long treks to search for sticks for fires, long lines to be given just enough to stay there. Nearly every meal was the same, but so valuable that the children in the pictures looked nearly wistful as they watched their mothers pick through those brown bags full of the only food their bellies had known.

In the beginning, I sat on the couch and pretended to like the food Jamila or her daughters cooked the few times it was offered to me. But it was obvious to anyone with eyes to see that I didn't value it like they did, how I wanted to talk through the meal and make friends with it, how I found it so interesting and fascinating, even as it was unpalatable to my tastes. It didn't mean that much to me, the rice and corn and beans, the bit of oil it was cooked in, the sugar sprinkled on top. It seemed only important as a gesture, a sign that I was fitting in, that I was going native. Jamila, I believe, knew this, and it did not sit well with her. And so when she stopped offering, it seemed almost natural.

The years passed. I started interacting more with the children, who were hungry for attention and in desperate need of help in school. I threw myself into these activities, for they helped me feel like the volunteer I was supposed to be. But I still showed up, every week, and sat on Jamila's couch, half-heartedly trying to have a conversation with her.

Every once in a while, she would call me on the phone. She would tell me that she needed to go to the store, and I would excitedly rush to my old, beat-up Toyota Corolla to come to her aid. And each time I showed up, she would load up my car with gigantic plastic bags filled with soda cans and beer bottles and ask me to return them for her. She always had a headache on these days and could never go with me. Her children, eager for a change of scenery, would beg to ride with me and so off we would all go, me fighting my mixed feelings (disappointed that Jamila wasn't coming with me, grateful that I was *helping* in a tangible way, annoyed that my car would now smell like old beer for the rest of the week), and we would stand around with the rest of the recycling crew—the post-homeless, the immigrants, the do-gooders. And I was never sure what category I fell in, exactly. I wanted to do good, sure. But wasn't there more to it than this? As we would leave, covered with sour and stale liquids, a few dollars clutched in our hands, I tried to console myself with the fact that I had just helped Jamila, in some small way.

At times, especially the first few years, it seemed the whole community was keeping one wary eye on me. I couldn't blame them, especially in the light of their traumatic pasts and current troubles. The initial pleasantries petered out into halfhearted waves, limp handshakes, a slight nod of recognition. When they stopped serving me chai when I showed up and instead just waved me in (never turning their gaze from WWE, which was always inexplicably on), when they stopped pretending to like what I cooked for them and spit out the food, when I slipped in the door like just another small child, I didn't mind these rejections. I would sit on the couch, surrounded by people I wasn't sure wanted me to be there at all, and I would feel serene and calm, as placid as a fern. All those years of dreaming and training to be a missionary, and here I was: ignored, used, and sitting in silence for long stretches of time.

It turns out that I am terrible at converting people the old-fashioned way, with logic and reasoning and concise tracts and fluid, poignant sermons. Instead, I have the much less interesting spiritual gift of showing up and sitting on couches, of doggedly arriving, gamely prepared to help in whatever crisis of the day, and eventually fading into a background player in a story that was turning out to be much bigger than me. Long after the enthrallment wore off, I found my heart had signed a commitment that led me to become deeply and irrevocably invested in the welfare of my friends, the poor in America. After several years, my friends and neighbors realized they were never going to get rid of me. The doors would be open a bit wider when I came around, I would be privileged to see both smiles and frowns, the reality of life that was so messy and moody and chaotic, instead of the nice and tidy one I wanted to see.

Still. If I am being honest, I continued to dream about those missionary heroes of mine, I still wanted to join their ranks. It would have been nice to have had a parade thrown for me every couple of years, hugs or tears or kisses maybe, a simple statue in the courtyard, a plaque on the front door. But I never arrived, never got a certificate, never got to check off the salvation of my friends on a neat and tidy chart. The years and years piled on top of one another, people halfheartedly leaving the door open a crack and me squeezing myself inside.

But Jamila now makes me chai every once in a while, which in its own way has a miraculous, festive air to it. I take whatever parades I can get.

I have a friend who has been living a much simpler, quieter, and ultimately more difficult life than I. One day I was complaining about an injustice I had received—how I had baked somebody some cookies, and they had refused to open the door to me. She looked at me, smiled for a split second, and then told me I should be grateful. "Grateful?" I said, not just the teensiest bit disgruntled. "Grateful for what?"

"That people feel the freedom to say no to you," she said, as if it were the most obvious thing in the world. "Be grateful they don't feel beholden to you in some way, be grateful that they are able to be authentic and to close a door in your face. Be grateful that you get to experience reality, instead of false politeness that can come from hierarchical relationships."

"Oh," my friend continued, "and you should be careful of your expectations. You expecting someone to open the door and accept your cookies is just another form of oppression. Just another person that wants something from them, is putting something on them, is expecting a certain reaction from them. Don't do that to them," my friend told me, no longer smiling. "They have had quite enough of that."

After my friend went home, I sat down and cried. Because all I ever wanted was for someone to say thanks. All I ever wanted was to hear "Well done, good and faithful servant." All I ever wanted was to be persecuted for righteousness's sake, to be a martyr for Jesus, to stoically endure doors slammed in my face, to persevere until the end.

But all I really ever wanted was to love on my terms, in a way that elevated me above my neighbor, distinguished me as good and holy, receiving accolades in a most humble way. All I ever wanted to do was oppress people, in the kindest way possible.

Three years after Hali was married, after I said goodbye in the chaos and thought I might never see her again, I am back in town visiting with her sisters, Saida and Khadija. They have both sprouted in my absence since I moved across the country the previous year. Khadija is tired of people telling her that she should play basketball. Saida is still the quiet one, but she also loves to giggle. I can't help but take pictures of them, but I dare not show them to the girls, especially Saida. She will frown and talk about how dark her skin is, how ugly her cheeks are. I can't bear to hear these words come out of her mouth, so I take the pictures and keep them to myself, hoarding the knowledge that these girls are so damn beautiful and I watched them grow up.

Not too much has changed. School is still hard. They have no friends, save for a few girls and boys that come from their particular tribe. Around the neighborhood, I see many other refugees and immigrants from East Africa—the glorious colors, the flowing head scarves, the throngs of children roaming the parks. I ask my girls why they don't talk to these other people, neighbors whom I assume would make good friends. The girls stare at me blankly, then answer as true as they know how: "They don't talk to us." And the conversation moves on, histories of oppressions and prejudices dismissed with an adolescent shrug. The girls have learned the hard way: they are on their own in the world.

We go out to eat Chinese food, where my husband makes them laugh and my toddler annoys them just slightly. They tell me that after all this time, Hali is coming back for a visit. "She's bringing her baby!" the girls tell me excitedly. Hali has a baby. One who can walk and talk, even. Her name is Aliya, and my mind draws a washed-out blank where I should be envisioning this child. But how can Hali have a baby? She is a baby herself.

At the park, after lunch, Saida tells me she does not expect to finish high school. Saida tells me that her mom recently realized she had gotten the dates wrong, that Saida was really seventeen, not sixteen. There is a boy she met on the Internet. He is a Bantu, like her. Maybe he will think she is beautiful.

History is repeating itself in front of my eyes. I wait for the hysterical feelings to come, but they don't. Of course she is too young, too vulnerable, too beautiful for this earth. But this is the story being told the world over, and I live two thousand miles away. All I can do is listen and wonder if this is what it means to grow older: the cruelties of the world are no longer surprising.

I make the girls promise to call me the second Hali lands. I will be in town visiting for a week longer, but I don't get my hopes up. I try not to think of anything at all.

Hali is there, in the living room, sitting with her baby in her lap. She smiles wide just like she always has. She has grown a bit too, wider in the ways that motherhood changes a person. Aliya is perfect, with kohl-rimmed eyes and necklaces of tiny black-and-white beads draped around her neck in order to ward off the *jin,* the evil spirits. She lets me hold her right away, which surprises me.

There are a lot of people crowded into the small living room, which is itself crowded with all the artifacts of the diaspora life: tapestries covering the walls, huge gilded couches taking up every wall. On one TV, Maury Povich is breaking up fights, on the other the video of Hali's wedding is playing on a loop. Men sprawl out on the couches, women and girls sit on the floor with babies crawling on their laps. Hali's uncle is painstakingly transcribing what he believes to be political missives about Somalia in English and is making Saida put them on Facebook. They are nonsensical to me, but the work is important to Mohammed.

Hali and I go to the kitchen, where she is cooking lunch for everyone. Pasta: tomatoes, onion, lots of oil and salt. It will be served with spaghetti noodles boiled to within an inch of their lives, topped off with a banana. I ask her about everything, and she answers me quick and clean. Did you finish high school? Yes, she says proudly, with a touch of defiance. How is your husband? Good. How is being a mom? Really good, and she smiles again. Do you have any friends? Yeah, she says, although there is no one like us there. Only my family and my husband's mom and sister. Other than that, there is no one. But I have other friends, she adds.

She tells me that she has a job, packaging makeup. Her

husband has a good job working for the Home Shopping Network. The American dream, come to life. She has another secret, one that she wants to tell me. "I'm going to college." It comes out fast. "The teachers say I can be an accountant. And when I am finished, they will help me find a job." I can't believe it, but Hali is as happy as I have ever seen her. Nineteen if she is a day, married, with a child, living far away from her family, isolated in a community where no one looks or acts or thinks like her. And in her own way, she is making it.

We wander into the next room, where I have my first conversation with her husband. His name is undecipherable to me, more African than the typical Islamic names I hear every day. He is a narrow man, very calm and relaxed. In his hands are fistfuls of bills and notices that he is carefully organizing for Jamila. He tells me all about the East Coast, and asks me quite a few questions about myself. He is reclining on his side on the couch, wearing a sarong wrapped around his waist. His thin fingers are reminiscent of Hali's father, whom I still miss. We sit in a collected happy silence, watching the children play at our feet. Life goes on, history repeats itself, and there are kindnesses to be found everywhere.

She'll be okay, I think to myself. She was never mine to protect anyway. And the God of the birds and bills and wedding cakes is watching with sharper eyes than mine. When it is time to leave, I hug everyone who will let me, and then let go. They were never mine to begin with.

I thought I was ministering to Jamila and her family all this time. But I found God by sitting on couches in the living rooms of people who grew up so differently from me. The more I showed up and sat on couches, the more I discovered that the good news of the kingdom of God came hand in hand with English lessons, malaria medication, WIC vouchers, and warm coats in winter. A God who cared about all the traumas and disappointments, who knew all the stories of my oppressed and enslaved and persecuted friends, a Jesus who came to set us all free, in our hearts and in our lives, from trying to earn the love of God.

Later, reading the gospels, I would see a Christ who was constantly interrupted by crisis, who had time for the people on the bottom of the pecking order, who always could be found in the wrong or just out-of-the-way apartments. And I fell in love with him. All because my friends opened up their doors to me, and let me sit on their couches.

Marigolds

In a tent in India, I'm seventeen years old, eating rice on a swept-clean dirt floor. The woman who cooked the meal for me is gaunt, with only several teeth intact. She looks much older than I assume she is, and her sari is colored with bright-green flowers. I eat her rice, mixed with a hot-as-hell curry composed of what looks to me like okra and not much else. I remember my dad telling me that spice is regularly used to disguise the taste of rotting vegetables, and I am suddenly grateful for the sweat that rolls off my brow.

Some of the family mills around, watching me and a few of my compatriots eat the rice and curry. Outside there is dust, cows, an idol shoved into the cracks at the base of the tree, orange marigolds in a chain around his neck. I eat my food with my right hand, as I have been taught. I squat awkwardly, used to a lifetime of sitting in chairs. I take the tall metal glass of water and drink it down, although I know I am not supposed to. I will pay for this later, all those exotic flora and fauna and bacteria bouncing around inside, but in the moment it feels like the right thing to do. What all those missionary heroes of mine would have done.

Since there is no common language, there is only the awkward sound of eating and the unsettling silence of being watched. The food tastes like fire, and I like it. We are in this tiny village to perform a play, with our trusty guide Bilal acting as our interpreter and preacher. Later, he will give an altar call, and no one will respond. When the sun goes down and there are no more lights, the village will have a changed look about it.

After the play (something about the temptations of money and women and alcohol, and how Jesus has the power to overcome them), late in the night, my team and I climb into a battered SUV and drive back to our flat in the city. On the way home, Bilal mentions the meal we ate inside the tent. "That was their one meal of the day," he said, in his beautifully lilting accent. "And they shared it with you." He turned his attention out the window, to the cool breeze coming in from the pockets of trees that we drove through. This was normal for him, this display of generosity. But for me, it was my first meal given to me by someone who would then do without; it was the first time I ate rice that was destined for another stomach. It was the first time I remembered the children milling around while we ate, the way their eyes watched our faces. It was their dinner we ate, pretending to be missionaries. The shame I felt tasted like bile, like heartburn that flared up angrily and dissolved into acid.

Later, I would remember the bright-green flowers, the way our hostess stirred with careful attention, the way the tent was so carefully swept and tidied. I would remember the water I drank, fetched from some faraway well. I would take the blessings of that meal with me much farther than the shame, once I was able to humble myself and accept the gifts being given to me all the time.

Later, in the few months I was in India, I would see other things that would cement these feelings. I would meet Christians whose faith was not tied up in their success (either economically or spiritually). I would meet people who would beam with happiness at the news of a God who loved them, of a Christ who came to take away sickness and fear. Workers who shared their tins of rice and curry on rooftops, teenage girls who whispered hopes and dreams for a future, children who cupped kittens in their hands and brought them to me to be kissed. Everyone, everyone, poor as far as my eyes could see. And yet, the generosity in which seemingly everyone moved changed me: how they adored bright colors and dramatic movies and soaring operatic songs and spicy food. Although it was deemed little by the world I had grown up in, it seemed to me that all of India was willing to share what they had.

Find your own Calcutta, Mother Teresa used to say, and in my fervor to become a missionary, I would read that and nod. Find, find, find my own Calcutta, probably somewhere in Africa, most definitely in the 10/40 window, unreached for sure, all the way, that's how I roll. In the future, when I am smarter and holier and know more. In three years, when I graduate with my degree in theology, when I will be able to explain all the points properly. In five years, when my debt is gone and I have found a team and a support system and am under the leadership of men with good doctrine in their heads and their hearts. In seven years, when doubt will no longer plague me and the words coming from my mouth will be magic, full of love and coercion, when people will be knocking my door over to be invited in for some seasonal, local, healthy food made with love. I will find my own Calcutta, for sure. I just have to make sure I am ready.

I grew up thinking that I could study my missionary heroes, saints, and role models, like Mother Teresa, enough to one day become them. I didn't realize that their theologies were a part of their bodies, the very lines in their faces, and that no book or teacher other than the very Spirit of God could give people the grace to do what they did. I studied Calcuttas all over the world and even visited for weeks and months at a time. But I wouldn't let them teach me. Instead, I looked to textbooks and seminaries and professors to tell me what to do with all the slums of our world. And whether I realized it or not, I absorbed the mindset that this Western method of education was the best way to go about doing anything: economically, socially, theologically. You go into debt, you learn from the best, and then you go out and be and teach and do with all that you have learned. And this isn't bad or wrong or untrue, not at all. Except for that one teeny tiny problem that I started to discover burrowed deep beneath all the years of enlightenment thinking that my culture and my church had swallowed like so much honey: Jesus never said those things.

But we say knowledge is truth, knowledge is superior, knowledge is power. Even though we don't mean to, our culture values education and right doctrine to the point that we have excluded the vast majority of the world. When did the lie come into the world that unless we were taught by brilliant, educated men we could never hope to understand what God's vision for the world was? When did we start to exclude the majority of people the world over from ever experiencing God? When did a building, a pastor, and even literacy skills become paramount for people to become disciples of Christ?

Perhaps when we stopped hanging out in Calcutta.

Perhaps Mother Teresa had a layered meaning for us. To be sure, in her Calcutta there were people dying every day: beggars, orphans, and widows. The poorest of the poor, they came to Mother to be bathed, clothed, and fed, and to die with dignity. There are comparable (although, as Dostoyevsky said, not similar) pockets of human need and desperation in every corner of the world. And in these margins of the Empire, far away from the institutions of learning and debating, people are experiencing God. They are encountering him, in big brick buildings and in apartment buildings, being washed by the Sisters of Charity or sharing stories with friends and family; the poor and the powerless have access to faith in ways the privileged can only dream about. They have the capacity to believe, regardless of the number of commentaries read or arguments made or sermons absorbed. They are the tiny grains of mustard that Jesus was so fond of, the widows, the orphans, the sick, and the crippled. Wherever Jesus went he was stopped by the people who never had a chance to study God from a distance; he was clutched at by the people whose desperation wasn't thinly veiled by power and position. He was interrupted and pursued and followed by those who were considered unclean and outcast, while the pure and the right made sure to keep their distance.

I was like a plaster cast of a saint, painted perfectly white and blue on the outside, for all the world to see. But on the inside, it was as gray and hollow as a tomb. It wasn't until I read the Bible with people who never had that I finally understood what "inspired Word of God" really meant. It wasn't until my three-year-old scraped her chin and asked me to pray for it to be healed, eyes screwed shut in anticipation of all pain being taken away, that I started to believe that "all things are possible with God." It wasn't until I was in a modest-looking living room full of somewhat damaged people singing awkwardly and off-key about the love of God that the phrase "the body of Christ" started to mean anything to me. Just like Nicodemus in the Bible, the church leader who came to talk to Jesus in the dead of night for fear of anyone seeing him, asked: "How can any of this possibly be?" How can God speak to thieves, murderers, rapists, and illiterates? How can God use broken, sick people to expand his vision for the world? How can the poor be the heralds of a new kingdom, one where education and power and creeds hold very little sway?

The truth is, most of the world will not have access to what I did: a Bible college, smart and humble professors, great thick books with creamy pages full of self-assured theology. But they have access to that one thing that I craved all along, what I paid good money for and spent years chasing after: the faith and assurance that God is present, he is involved, and he loves them.

When I was seventeen, in India for the first time, closer to death, disease, and persecution than I had ever been, I saw a bit of this kingdom. And I went home on an airplane feeling confused at the wells of gratitude and generosity I had found. The imprint of God, the world over, stunning me with the realization that the poor are blessed to see in ways I never would. While I live my life hoarding all that I have been given—privilege, opportunity, right beliefs and doctrines—there are people all around the world offering up their last meal. Take it, they say, although they have no knowledge of what the next day will bring.

And that's exactly where the kingdom of God flourishes like a marigold in a dry stream, a flash of gold in the dirt of our world. Blessed are those with eyes to see it; blessed are those who will do anything to experience more of it. I've been trying to find those flashes ever since.

I was once asked to make a list of my life, to compile the highs and the lows on a neat little chart.

It first happened at a postmodern sort of conference, the kind where the purpose is strangely murky and different speakers give pep talks and show pictures of the amazing things they have done. I am left wondering what the hell I have done with my life, wasting my salad years on college and finding myself and hanging out with assorted random friends when I could have been pioneering microloans for women in India. On the plus side, at the beginning of the conference I received an understated brown binder made out of recycled materials, complete with a graph-paper chart to plot out the story of my life. There were pages for me to write about major characters, roles, turning points, recurring and central themes. I was into it. I got all Oprah-y, ready to dig down deep, ready to start thinking about living my best life now. And then, right in the middle of projecting my own goals for the future, the main speaker of the event paused his "session" and looked me right in the eye. "Some of you are sitting here, thinking: I'm special." He stopped for a moment, and the room got very still. "Is that you? Do you hear that still small voice inside of you? That you are destined for great things?" He stopped again, and we all looked at him, The Famous Christian Author, as he went on: "Because I am here to tell you—it's true. Some of you are born to be special."

Almost as an afterthought, he added: "Which, of course, means some of you are not."

As I held my binder in my hand, my pathetic few ups and downs already penciled into the chart, the "turning points" in my non-memoir-worthy life all laid out, my soul jumped forth. *It was me,* I thought. *I am one of the special ones.* I guess I had known all along, and I just needed someone—a middle-aged, successful Christian author—to pinpoint what had been poured into my bones. I was special.

I looked around, furtively. I had essentially sneaked into this conference, had been given a free ticket purely by chance. I didn't know anyone here, and I was too tired from the complexities of work and child rearing and life to put any effort into my appearance, nor any real thoughtfulness into the "work" of the conference. I was surrounded by good-looking young people, all wearing brown boots. I was surrounded by warm-hearted grandmothers, ready to write about themselves for the first time. I was surrounded by hip but slightly disillusioned youth pastors, desperate for some relevant good news to go back and share on the front lines. I looked around and I thought: *Do you all know who he's talking about? Yeah, it's me.*

But before I could delve too deeply into that well, I noticed something. People all around the auditorium were sitting up straighter. Heads were cocked to the side, eyes bright and looking forward, pens poised above life plans. There was a stillness in the room, one that made me suddenly and acutely aware that none of us believed that we weren't one of the special ones. All of us believed we were the rare birds, the undiscovered geniuses, the next big thing waiting to happen. And I quickly slumped back into my own chair, ashamed at my own thoughts. All of us had that still small voice inside of us, I realized. But we can't all be that special.

I went back to penciling in the highs and the lows, more

than a little embarrassed by my own deep wells of narcissism. And when I came to the last page of the binder ("What is the Theme of Your Life?") I left it blank. *Wouldn't it be nice*, I thought, *if any of us actually knew the answer to that one? Wouldn't it be lovely if good stories could be lived out just by attending a conference? Wouldn't it be grand, if it was as simple as someone reminding us all how special we really were?*

The list of my life lay untouched for a year or two, until my small family and I sold all of our possessions and moved across the country, joining a mission organization that works and lives among the urban poor. We wanted to learn from people who were better than us at loving their neighbors in the margins of America. It sounds all super-sexy and like you may live out the nice, missionary version of *The Wire* until you find yourself alone and friendless in your hovel of an apartment, cooped up by the mountains of snow and the screaming of your neighbors, listening to your two-year-old get called a racist on a daily basis, constantly wondering if you are supposed to call the cops or invite someone over for dinner, and completely overwhelmed by your inability to do anything of lasting relational importance. When I was asked to make a life list to share with my team-mates in my mission organization, five months into our first year, I was having the I-Am-Special shit kicked out of me on a daily basis. And it made for a better list.

This time I laid awake at night and thought about what really should go on my list. What were the real ups and downs, the actual experiences that changed me for good and for bad? What were the real negatives, the words and actions and experiences that sunk deep inside my soul? I was surprised by what I found. The memories that were sharp enough to cut were those that swam out of the deep, quiet hours of the morning. The spiritual leaders and their crippling words passing judgment on a girl who was thirsty for holiness. The traumas of illness and near death and premature birth. The sermons and teachings on women in leadership that left me dizzy with anger and sadness, shaking for fear that it was true that God loved some more than others.

There was the good stuff too: a childhood marked by my belief in a very good God, the trips around the world where I discovered my strong and uncompromising nature, my ability to find joy in the unknown and uncomfortable. There was meeting my husband, shyly surrendering to a life lived for two. There were the times I met new friends from foreign worlds, neighbors who opened up worlds on the margins that I never knew existed and changed me with their stories and lives and friendships.

But what were the lies? I tried to look out for them, those beliefs that had seeped in around the edges after years of striving hard after God. I saw the highlights reel of my life. I saw the parts that I most badly wanted others to see: starting programs for the under-resourced, moving into apartment complexes, moving across the country to do more and to do it better. And beneath all of that seemingly "good" stuff was a girl who had placed herself on a pedestal, someone who believed *I am destined for something special, because I am special.*

Those books about my heroes only reinforced this, as did my Christian culture around me. There are some people who go out and do Big Things for God, and I knew in my heart that I just happened to be one of them. And it was unspoken, of course, but the flip side of this belief was an ugly little hierarchy, a drive to be out on the top that came more from desperation than idealism: *I am special because I have to be. Because God loves the special more.*

I didn't start to notice this real and powerful lie, this dark animal clawing up my mind, until it almost undid me. I didn't see how I placed myself at the top and was eager for others to do the same. I didn't see how that meant that my neighbors and refugee friends became my stepping stones in attaining the love of God; I didn't see how it meant that I was using everyone around me in real and devastating ways.

But in the strange way that freedom comes, the worse my life started to look on paper, the more I started to find the God I had been looking for all of my life. The more I failed and the more overwhelmed I was by the world, the more I started to inch toward a place of accepting radical grace for myself. Far away from inspirational conferences, getting my gentrifier, do-gooder ass handed to me on a daily basis, I was finally in a place to look at my life in a more honest way. And it was becoming increasingly clear that there wasn't even a bit of specialness to be found in me, and that God loved me anyway.

Idols

Once I took a group of refugees from Bhutan to the ocean. It was supposed to be a nice, pleasant picnic. Everyone brought food to share, and my husband and I and a few friends drove our cars, caravanning to the waves. It was windy, but beautiful and clear. We found picnic tables covered by an awning and started to unpack the food—chicken legs, watermelon, and sprinkle-covered cookies that I had made. But before we all started tucking into the food, the crowd of families we had brought started to head toward the water. I assumed they wanted to see it, touch it, rejoice in the glory of the ocean before we got down to the business of eating, talking, and laughing. But I was surprised when the women started pulling out apples and incense and lighters, as they started to perform ceremonies that I had no frame of reference for.

In my memory they took paper plates and placed an apple in the middle of each, sticking three or four sticks of incense into each apple. I can't be sure, but it seems like some of them brought flowers, perhaps plastic, to scatter on the plates. They found a tributary, a shallow-yet-fast river that was racing to meet up with the ocean. And my friends and neighbors—old women in saris, young children in flip-flops, middle-aged men wearing ski caps to protect them from the ocean chill—started sending their paper plates full of fragrant apples out to sea.

I watched, mesmerized, from the sidelines. It was some sort

of sacrifice to the gods of the ocean. We huddled close together and watched the apples bob along the water. One plate caught on fire but quickly sank in a glob of ash before I could panic. Tourists, walking past, gave us all extremely strange looks. But my friends, they watched their little lights head off into the great blue yonder until we could see them no more. I don't know if they were trying to appease anybody. I don't know if they thought it would make their lives back at home any easier, if those little sticks of incense could help pay the bills, could find good-paying jobs, could help their children do better in school. Perhaps they just wanted to say thank you for the gift of the water. Whatever the case, the gesture was a sobering one for me.

I had forgotten, was the thing. How so many around the world live connected to this sense of the spirits around us, the circles of sacrifice and blessing, in a transparent system of religion where one seeks to even the odds, to control a bit of the divine. And I envied them, my friends, just the tiniest bit on the beach that day. At least they were extremely forthright about their idols, about all the ways we try so hard to make the odds be in our favor.

I was raised to look for passages about idolatry, the premier sin of the Old Testament. Compromise was a major theme of my young life, trying hard to keep clean hands and a pure heart, prayer and Bible times, and careful journaling in the morning. My culture focused on the aesthetics: modest dress, an absence of narcotics, sweet words that differentiated us from the foul and the popular. Christian culture in my childhood and teen years was primarily characterized by shying away from the idolatries of the secular: movies, music, clothes. We categorized ourselves by what movies we didn't watch, what music we didn't let grace our ears, whether or not a slip of our backside showed as we sat down in folding chairs to hear the Word of God. We were trying very hard to be holy, and we had to shut most of the world out in order to do so.

The Bible has become a slippery thing for me now. The words on the page have started to swim in front of my eyes. It's like reading Arabic, from the right to the left, these days, with everything upside down. How could I have missed it in the Old Testament, the psalms, the laments, the prophets, the very narrative of the Israelites, the gospels, the letters of Paul, the culmination of Revelation? Oppressed peoples are a theme, those downtrodden by life, circumstances, the wicked, and the unjust. And the promise, always the promise, of God delivering justice. Sometimes it was a strange, terrible kingdom doing the oppressing: the exotic Assyrians, the people choked with gold and false gods with a hunger for land and for bodies. Sometimes it was the Lord's own people acting in wicked ways, taxing the poor, crushing them, getting fat and wealthy while others in their own community withered away. This is when the wrath and sorrow of God seemed most mixed together, mingling like the blood and water would centuries later, when God put on flesh, inaugurated his kingdom.

So now, to approach that living Word, those long-ago thoughts that keep shifting before my eyes and causing me to see something new every morning, I am confused. Yes, there is still talk about golden calves and statues of the Baal, temples built and offerings burned, but these visuals all are starting to take a backseat to other issues: the hearts of the people of God—their greed, lust for power or people, their condescension, their preoccupation with themselves. Like me and everyone I know, they are obsessed with staying safe and securing a good life for themselves, protecting their borders and procuring a retirement account. Sometimes they believe that obeying God will lead to this good life; sometimes they are right. Sometimes they believe that copying other countries, adopting their ways, will bring about material blessing. This works, sometimes, for short periods of time. But the scriptures show us time and time again what these ways of living spell out, what the first signs of sin and idolatry are: the poor are forgotten, they are downtrodden and oppressed.

I looked at the pages of the Bible with thousands of years of hindsight, perfectly content to read the sins of another age into it. Those people loved other gods, slept with women of different faiths, put arrows in each other's backs, were consumed with jealousy over friends and lovers, worshipped the things of gold, bowed down before terrible statues, and flaunted their sins in the eyes of God. We read this, collectively, clucking our tongues. We waved away our own sins—materialism, gluttony, greed—as merely obnoxious distractions, a fly in our relatively holy faces. We were nothing like the people of the Old Testament, and we were grateful. Thank God that chapter in history is over. But is it? I have been going back and rereading the stories, the narratives, the prophets, and the songs. And the things that caused the wrath and tears of God are the same today: injustice.

The God of my youth, who when people spoke of him sometimes seemed more like an oppressor, someone who doled out punitive punishments like candy, who was always waiting for the next terrible thing to happen, has changed in my eyes. I see now a sorrowful, hopeful God. One who, no doubt, was exasperated by all the idolatry and murmurings and wanderings and complaining, but whose wrath was directly stoked by oppression. I see how he was the tireless advocate of the poor, the widow, and the orphan. How he saw, time and time again, that these were the first to be forgotten, a sign that the hearts of the people were far from him, even if they weren't quite yet bowing down to Baal. As we see again and again in scripture, righteousness is not simply a clean heart or hands scrubbed of blood. It is a people acting out justice in their everyday lives; they are tied together, everywhere in scripture. The oppressed are written in every book, nearly on every page of the prophets and psalms. How could I have missed it for so many years?

I was untouched by money, alcohol, sex, drugs, and rock 'n' roll. I was an obedient Israelite, no idols hidden in my closet, nothing of gold or silver or bronze or stone that I worshipped. Always a strange child, from a very young age all I wanted was to see the face of God, just like Moses did. I wanted my face to glow in the same way, bright as the sun, so that others would have to look away.

Only an oppressor could be so blind. But thanks to the surprising relationships I have been blessed with, my eyes are slowly starting to see.

There is a knock on the door, and it startles me. I am trying to cook dinner, and it is very hot in my ground-level apartment. We had just moved in, we were returning to the Pacific Northwest after being gone for three years. We picked an apartment complex on the far outer edges of the city of Portland, because that's where the cheapest rent was. Our neighbors are mostly refugees and immigrants, and it is an incredibly diverse blip in otherwise homogenous Portland. In our complex alone, over eighty languages are spoken.

There is a knock on the door, and my daughter races to open it. I follow right behind her, holding the baby on my hip. When we open the door there are three teenagers standing there: two girls and a boy. They smile and talk in a rush: "Hi, we are having a Bible club out in the courtyard and wanted to know if you had any kids that wanted to come?" I am dumbfounded. For a minute, I just stare at these visions of youthful goodwill. The girls are wearing long skirts and T-shirts advertising their youth group; the boy is wearing cargo shorts and flip-flops. I look into their faces, and they are serene. They don't seem nervous, or agitated. They are very comfortable with what they are doing, or else they are very good at faking it.

I stammer something out to them—"sure, maybe we will check it out"—and my daughter is clinging to my knees, asking to go, my baby is starting to cry, and I can feel the sweat running down my back. They push a flier into my hands and smile at me and they move on to the next apartment.

I am taken outside of my body. What do I look like to them? Do I look like I belong? My daughter is in preschool, and her hair is wild and messy and her clothes are mismatched. *They probably think she is poor,* I realize with a start. *They probably think she needs evangelizing.* I live in one of the run-down apartment complexes on the edges of the city, the ones where people are barely treading water: the type of complex where you deliver food boxes at Thanksgiving, where you deliver presents at Christmas, where you drive a big blue van up once a week called "The Bible Bus" and help all those poor, needy children.

I want to ask these bright young things, "Do you know I used to do that too?" Instead, I throw on more presentable clothes, strap my baby to my chest, and take my daughter out back into the middle of the courtyard so we can experience the Bible club together. My daughter loves it. An awkward thirteen-year-old paints a Disney princess on her arm. There are kids playing soccer with some gangly older boys. There is a little water station, and animal cookies, and on a tree stump I see a young volunteer laying out the story of the gospel for two children using a cube, each side telling a different section of the garden-fall-sin-redemption story.

I hang out in the back, hovering close enough to keep an eye on my daughter. Some of the kids think I am leading the club, however, due to my skin color. I hurriedly assure them that no, I'm not leading it. Just observing. But they don't believe me. The Bible club kids start performing a skit, and they are so good at it. Loud, funny, assured—something about a little boy who lies, who doesn't listen to his parents, who is disrespectful to his teacher at school. The kids laugh and laugh at the teenager who is pretending to be a naughty little boy, how he sticks out his tongue and huffs around in annoyance and anger. My daughter's face could split with delight, her blond hair bobbing amid the sea of black and brown around her.

There is a teenager with short hair and an intense air about her, and she is the teacher of the group. After the skit, she explains what it means to the kids. She holds up a white cloth heart, and she starts to pour a rusty brown liquid onto it. As she goes over all the bad things that the naughty boy did throughout his day, the white heart gets dirtier and dirtier. This is what sin does, she says calmly to all those children. This is what your heart looks like to God when you sin.

My own spirit shrinks within me. I drift off into my mind. I think about what I used to believe about God, how I tried so hard to make myself clean and pure and told others to do the same. Now I think about these kids, and I know just a tiny bit of the troubles they may be facing in their small lives—the financial instability, the rent hikes, the lack of nutritious food, the bullying at school, the ways they have to navigate the world for their parents, the ways they have been forced to grow up much too soon. The teacher leads the kids in a prayer of repentance, and then everyone is off to run wild in the grass.

These pious teenagers told the whole gospel story exactly right, just as they had been taught it. I want to feel kindly toward them, to applaud the earnestness and the faith. I think that maybe these kids enjoy it; maybe it is a fun hour to run and take a break from real life; maybe it is all for the best. But we go back home, and my daughter wants to talk about black hearts for the rest of the evening. She wants to know how dirty she appears before God. I think back to the first time she heard the story of David and Goliath, how troubled she was, how her eyes glanced off the page of the large, fallen giant and turned to pierce me with their confusion. "Didn't God love Goliath?" she asked me, and her childlike faith started to unravel something within me. *Didn't God love all of these kids, our neighbors, their parents, the whole world?* Did he look at them and see black hearts, spotted with rust, the ones on the bad side of the story? Or does he look at them and see pieces of himself, millions of bright red and raw hearts wandering around the earth?

I do not let my daughter go back to the Bible club all week long that summer. I think my aggrieved thoughts to myself. *If I were them*, I say, forgetting that I was, and still am, one and the same as those beautiful, confident souls. *If I were them, I would focus a bit more on the love of God. That's what these kids need to hear.* But when I was their age, a delightfully confident bright young thing, I wouldn't have been able to talk about the real love of God because I didn't know what it was. And the paradox has been, the more I have discovered this love for myself, the harder it has become to share it on a bracelet, or in a skit, or in a sermon. The love has quieted me, confused me, and dragged me into places I never could have foreseen. It cannot be tamed, and that is turning out to be very inconvenient indeed.

After that Bible club in my backyard, I thought about what my daughter had said and how twisted up my insides got as I tried to answer. I thought about the Bible, the story of God, as a whole. It is not, as a preacher I recently heard say, a book about people living their best life now. David, the one who killed Goliath, the hero of that story, stuck out in my mind especially. That night, I worked over the basics of his story, over and over again. How he started off young and free in the pastures with his sheep, steeped in the wilderness and the love of God. How he went on to be prophesied over, to be hunted for sport, to become a great king and then a terrible one. I thought of his life—the rape, the murder, the blood-stained hands, the terrible parenting decisions—and I remember how God had said David was a man after his own heart, a man through whom the Christ would come.

I thought about David, young and alone, singing songs to his sheep, completely surrounded by the presence of God. I thought of David, old and sad and ready to go home, completely surrounded by the presence of God. I read his psalms, his songs of lament, praise, and damnation, and I was astonished at the scope of them. David could say whatever he wanted, could bring his erratic, moody, giddy, and unwell self to the table— because he knew God loved him.

And I was angry, my heart a flame of indignation and jealousy and something that very much felt like sorrow. For if God could truly delight in a person like David, then why was I trying so damn hard? It was because I never believed I had earned his love after all.

But like the smallest of seeds, an idea began to grow: What if it was all true? What if God loved everybody, exactly the same? What if there were no hierarchies, no gold stars, no way to spill or waste or fritter away or lose the love of the Almighty? In my mind, based on my experiences, I was beginning to understand what the scriptures said, what the prophets and the poets fleshed out constantly: God loved the poor and powerless, the ones who weep and are abused. He loves the damaged ones, the bruised reeds, the trampled, and the forgotten. This, this I could believe. But the Bible also talked extensively about those on the other side, and it was still all love. His forgiveness is astounding, beyond comprehension. The idea lodged itself in my heart, and I could not look away: God also loves the oppressors, the abusers, the young people with savior complexes, the gluttons, and the cowards. He loves us all so much, that he cannot help but bring his kingdom. He gives his woes and blessings alike, all out of love. There is no one that can be left out; the door is wide open to whoever should enter.

When I asked God about all this, he told me some hard and true things, which amounted to what I had heard my whole life but didn't have the wherewithal to actually believe: God loves everybody, exactly the same. No matter what you do.

If you grew up like me, then you are waiting for the asterisk to that sentence. Sure, God loves everybody the same. *But he *really* likes it when you go to Africa. Or start a food kitchen. Or adopt through foster care. Or buy cool, overpriced shoes that may or may not give an orphan in some nameless country a complimentary pair. Or turn your TV into a garden for succulents. Or whatever it is that we believe we must do in order to be fully loved.

God took away my asterisk, and now I don't know how to classify myself anymore. I'm just a sheep of his hand, and it is more lowly and lovely than I could have ever imagined.

The Ministry of Cake

I once had a student named Anis, who was trying very hard to make it in America. He had five children and another on the way, and his wife was very sick. Anis came faithfully to my English class, the lone male in a sea of strong women, because he wanted to learn English and get a good job. The women in my class tormented him mercilessly, always volunteering him to go up to the whiteboard and write his sentences. Anis, henpecked and harried, would go to the front and stand in front of the board. He would turn to me and smile. "Teacher," he would say, and then he would just laugh. He could not write the sentences on the board, because he had never learned to read or write in any language, and besides—he had much larger problems on his mind.

Anis did not have a driver's license, yet he somehow managed to procure beat-up old vans and go careening around the city. He would pick up other people and take them to appointments, he took women living at the shelter to go grocery shopping, he scouted out possible job leads at the airport, he drove to my class. Once, he showed me fistfuls of crumpled-up traffic citations, and he had no idea what they were. One day his wife went into labor, and my other students came in and told me how Anis had lost his mind in the ensuing panic. He drove like a crazy man, and the police arrested him for a day. Now he does not know where his car is; this is why he is not at class. A few days later, there he was, showing me pictures of his new daughter. I pleaded with him, I scolded him sternly. "Stop driving!" And he would just smile, and nod his head. "Yes, Teacher."

One day we had a class party. Since there were so few tangible gains made in the area of actual literacy in English, we celebrated every little old thing. Someone was finally able to spell her own name, somebody got a job, somebody had a delicious little baby, somebody found stable housing, somebody's daughter was getting married. Every few months, I made sure we had a party. People brought in food that they cooked themselves, all of it amazing, and I usually brought in some cupcakes and soda.

Anis came to the party and brought his oldest son, a shy eleven-year-old I had met when I had gone to their house to visit one day. They brought a surprise for me. It was a gigantic sheet cake from a bakery, covered with pillows of white frosting and surrounded by black roses. "Congrtulations [sic] for Graduating," it said in a loopy black cursive. "Teacher, Teacher, it is for you." Anis was smiling at me, and all the students clapped their hands. I stared down at that glorious cake, and I wanted to both laugh and cry. Anis's son sidled up to me. "I picked it out," he whispered. "I'm the one who told them what to write." It was perfect, and I told him as much. We loaded up our plates with food, and we all took large squares of that cake. We smiled at each other, our teeth blackened by the food coloring, me and Anis's son the only ones who could understand what was written on the cake, none of us ever in danger of graduating anything, and all of us understanding how good it was to be together.

Anis, fresh off of a night in jail, loaded up his car with women of the class and proceeded to take them all to their homes. He smiled at me as he drove away, and I thought to myself: *Now there is a guy who has not let life beat him down. Now there is a guy who is committed to finding moments of celebration wherever he goes.*

In my life, I have baked a thousand cakes.

No matter where I find myself—a fancy baby shower, an English class, an apartment-wide BBQ, a Bible study, even at weddings and funerals and wakes—I bring baked goods. Pies, chocolate cakes, seasonal galettes, rustic fruit tarts—sugar, butter, comfort. It's my testimony to the good in the world. I seek out the sweet in the midst of all the bitter. More than anything, though, I find myself reaching for a box of Funfetti cake mix, full of rainbow-colored sprinkles, just like my mom used to make me. Funfetti cupcakes, much like spicy hot Cheetos and Orange Fanta, have been the consistent crowd-pleasers in my life, a true cross-cultural phenomenon. Every excuse for a celebration, every chance for commiseration, and I am in my kitchen, baking out my feelings.

The other day I found myself making yet another batch of cupcakes, late at night, for a neighbor of mine who was moving away. Her story is sad and as ancient as could be: bruises on her cheeks, a broken ankle, an apologetic cast to her eyes. She was moving away to be with a man I was sure was the cause of all her hurts and bruises, and I could barely swallow as I stirred my cupcake batter, sprinkled with red and green and blue bits. A few other neighbors and I went and gave her the cake, and we sat on a mattress in the middle of her bare apartment and ate our Funfetti.

We said goodbye, and I went back to my own place. And I tossed and turned and talked to God, asking, how much more of this I could handle. How many cakes can I bake for people who move away? Who make terrible choices, who have horrible things happen to them? What do I do with all of these great, gaping souls shuffling around, their bruised cheeks and downcast eyes haunting me, begging the question: How much of this can God take? How much longer can I keep making these damn cupcakes?

Jesus, speaker of parables, told a famous story once. It's about a prodigal boy—shaming his father, running off with the hoodlums, squandering his money, promise, and talent. Ashamed, he heads home, despondent, intent on being a field hand in his father's house. But the father has been waiting the whole time, searching the horizon for any sight of his boy. When he catches a glimpse of his son, the father eschews all dignity and runs madly down the dirt roads, hugging him "while he was still a long way off." I have always loved the beauty of this story, the way it presents a grace-filled father with strong eyes and arms, someone who is looking actively for the redemption of all of his prodigals. When I read this story to my daughter at night, straight out of the *Jesus Storybook Bible,* I cry, every time.

The problem was, I was never the prodigal. I was never a long way off, never strayed from the fold. I was born in the church, schooled in the church, and imagined myself to die a saint-like death in the church. And since I never left the Father, it never felt like he was looking for me.

This was the story we were told as children, all emphasis placed on the prodigal. But when I was older, I read the story for myself and was shocked to find that I *was* in there. In the story there is another character, often left out in the Sunday school lessons. He is the older brother, the one who works the fields and obeys his father tirelessly. He never squanders anything, just obeys and obeys and obeys. And all the while, his heart is souring, his own spirit yearning to be sought after.

When the prodigal returns home, the father throws a big party (just like God would; I am beginning to learn in slow and small ways how much God loves good food and celebration, when I thought he just loved work). The older brother is affronted and refuses to go into the party. "It's not fair," he shouts, listing off all the ways he has been the good son. "Why isn't there a party for me?" He echoes the same sentiment that I have found myself often wondering: Why don't I get to experience any of the good things? Where are my converts? My miracles? My blessings, my anxiety-free days, my table full of food and friends and a Father God who is cutting the cake for me? I don't see it anywhere. I am stuck in the far-off fields, toiling away for a Father who has seemingly forgotten about me.

At church the other day, my pastor was preaching on this very parable, one I had not thought of in a long time. When he got to the end of the story, my pastor read about how the father left the party to go speak to the older brother, who was still refusing to enter into the celebration. The resentment oozed out of his pores, this older brother who didn't know how he could do anything more to earn his father's love, to receive a party of his own. The father, full of sadness and mercy, tells his older son—so good, so bitter—a simple thing. "My son," he says, looking the boy full in the eyes. "You are always with me, and everything I have is available to you." He doesn't need to add what by now I knew: it was always available to him, all along. Being near the Father is a constant party-in-progress, a constant chance to experience the benefits of being in community. But we can choose to opt out of it, to work tirelessly for an idea of what our Father wants, instead of spending time with him.

Those words, ones I must have heard from childhood but had long since forgotten, will never leave me again. All that I have, says the God of the world, is available to you. And it always has been.

You just need to sit down and enjoy the party.

Some of the most unrecognized ministries are my favorite kind.

Like the ministry of playing video games with awkward adolescent boys. The ministry of bringing takeout food to people whose baby is very sick in the hospital. The ministry of picking up empty chip wrappers at the park. The ministry of sending postcards. The ministry of sitting in silence with someone in the psych ward. The ministry of sending hilarious and inspirational text messages. The ministry of washing dishes without being asked. The ministry of flower gardening. The ministry of not laughing at teenagers when they talk about their relationship crises. The ministry of making an excellent cup of coffee. The ministry of drinking a terrible cup of coffee with a bright smile. The ministry of noticing beauty everywhere—in fabrics, in people, in art, and in the wilderness.

The older I get, the more I realize that the ministries I once thought so trivial I now think are the most radical. I have spent the past few years being stripped of anything that would make me feel lovely to God, and I came out a different person. As it turns out, I never did magically turn into one of my missionary heroes. Instead, I'm just somebody who likes to bake cakes.

I used to want to witness to people, to tell them the story of God in digestible pieces, to win them over to my side. But more and more I am hearing the still small voice calling me to *be* the witness. To live in proximity to pain and suffering and injustice instead of high-tailing it to a more calm and isolated life. To live with eyes wide open on the edges of our world, the margins of our society. To taste the diaspora, the longing, the suffering, the joy. To plant myself in a place where I am forced to confront the fact that my reality is not the reality of my neighbors. And to realize that nothing is how it should be, the ultimate true reality of what God's dream for the world is.

Being a witness is harder than anything I have ever done. And he is asking all of us to do this task, to simultaneously see the realities of our broken world and testify to the truth that all is not well. To be a witness to the tragedy, to be a witness to the beauty. Jesus, the ultimate witness of the love of the Father, heart of God, shows us the way. He put himself in situations where he was constantly confronted with brokenness: death, disease, sickness, greed, pride. And Jesus ran toward those people, so confident was he in a God who sees.

I am starting to believe in this love, with Jesus as my example. He sought out the stateless wanderers, the exiles, the people with stories so sad and unfair, the ones who were the most receptive to his message that another world was possible. He has asked me to be a witness to those same kinds of people, and in return I have experienced a faith in God that could never be taught.

I see it all, the God of the scriptures says over and over again. I see it all, and my heart is torn in two. And he is asking people like me, the very nonspecial, the bakers and the questioners and the fretful sleepers, to allow ourselves to see it all too. The prodigals and the older brothers, the lost sheep and the sheep who were too scared to ever leave the pen. There is a place for us all here, the call for all of us to be present and be a witness to the realities of the world. To live in a place where neighbors will move away, again and again and again, to keep showing up on couches and sitting wide-eyed, to sit and say "I'm sorry."

He is asking us to drop everything and run, run in the direction of the world's brokenness. And he is asking us to bring cake.

The older brother is the real prodigal, the one who starved in the middle of the feast. Too brittle with resentment and trying to earn God's love, too busy creating a hierarchy where he came out on top that he missed out on all that was available to him.

His story is my story, and it might be yours too.

I am here as living proof that it is all available to us, and it has been this whole time. All those blessings, just like Jesus talked about. We just need to be in relationship with those to whom Jesus said the miracles of the kingdom would come: the poor, the sick, the sad, the oppressed.

Like many of our stateless wanderer friends, my little family and I have moved a few times. And each time we pack up our apartment, my refugee friends and neighbors bring gifts: clothes for the toddler, fried fish cooked whole and sliced like a baguette, crumpled dollar bills that they shove into my shirt. Before, I would have felt ashamed, unworthy, like I could have done more. Now, I weep with relief, with the blessings of being loved. As my friends offer to help clean and pack and take many of our worldly goods back to their own apartments, it feels good, even authentic, to be the recipient. To be the one in need. It confirms that this is quite possibly the only posture that Christians in this day and age can take, to be in a place where we freely admit our shortcomings, where we desperately need our neighbors. A place where we throw off the voices telling us to insulate ourselves from both the great brokenness of the world and the burning fire that is the love of God.

Perhaps, in the decades to come, people will look back and wonder how all of this was possible, for great wealth and great poverty to exist, side by side, for so very long. For people to sing songs about God's love while wearing a shirt made by slaves. For people to spend all their time describing or taming God, trying to convince everyone else that this is the only way it ever could be.

The great lie of our time is that the kingdom of God is not at hand and that it isn't ever coming. That inequality, sadness, destruction, and death are inevitable. That we must either despair or escape in the relief of busy and separate lives, succumb to fear or to apathy.

But I've seen it with my own eyes, touched it with my hands. I've moved in next door to it and traveled to the suburbs to experience it. Everything Jesus ever said is true, not just the parts I want to believe.

His kingdom is here. It's the cup of cold water in a village in India. The first and last story ever written by Abdi. The pastor who prays for people to be healed and the little girl who dreams of sailing away to foreign countries. The awkward parties where people come in spite of everything. He is the babies that were saved and the babies that were lost. The cakes you bake for neighbors moving away into very bad situations and the bags of cans you turn in for change. Christ is everywhere, in everything small, every blade of grass, every kindness you ever received. He is the only song you've ever heard that made sense. He sees blessing where everyone else sees only a curse. He is love—that's all he ever was and all he ever will be. His heart is aflame, and he will wound you and heal you at the same time.

The world is so much worse than we would like to believe, and God is so much wilder than we are being taught. We can study the kingdom of God, but we can never contain or subdue it. Reading about it will never equal the experience of it. That we must discover for ourselves, and we will find it where God always said it would be: on the margins, in the upside-down kingdom. We aren't being asked to assimilate, but we are called to make our home here more like the kingdom we have always dreamed about but were too scared to believe was possible. Because God's dream for the world is coming, looming brighter and brighter on the horizon.

It's time to enter the party.

Acknowledgments

First of all I want to thank Krispin, my husband, the king of the unrecognized ministries. Without you there would be no story and certainly no book. You make me feel less alone in the world, and also you are adorable. I must also thank my children, who made it both essential and impossible to write. The kingdom is coming through you! Mama loves you! To my parents, for raising me with a thirsty heart, a sense of love and safety, and eyes to see the kingdom all around: I am so grateful to you. To my sisters, Lindsay and Candyce, my best friends, you keep me young, and humble, and I love you.

My thanks go to my writing group that became my lifeline: Amy Lepine, Kelley Nikondeha, Jessica Goudeau, Christiana Peterson, Stina Kielsmeier-Cook—you are my listening ears and angel editors and kick-ass cheerleaders. Without you this book would have been 100% awful. Thank you also to Martyn Jones, Claire Deberg, Kelsey Maddox, Janelle Hosfield, and my mom Shawn Strannigan for reading through various sections and editions of the manuscript and for your invaluable feedback.

Thank you to John Warner at McSweeney's, for being the first editor to give me a chance and for publishing my desperate, amateur thoughts. Portions of the following essays were originally published at Timothy McSweeney's Internet Tendency: "Stateless Wanderers," "Light and Dark," "Vacation Bible Schools," "The Kingdom of Heaven," "Refugeed," "The

Wedding," "Wade in the Water," and "On Motherhood, On Death." To Greg Wolf for picking the essay "The Rule of Life" out of the slush pile and publishing it in *Image Journal* (vol. 82). To the editors who worked with me and pushed me and published me: John Wilson, Richard Clark, Alan Noble, Matthew Shedden, Katelyn Beaty, Adam Joyce, Tyler Glodjo, Nicole Cliffe, and Kate Shellnutt.

Thank you to the writers out there who inspired and encouraged me, both in their books and in real life, especially Jonathan Wilson-Hartgrove. His kindness and humility in the face of long-term activism are nothing short of amazing. To Shane Claiborne and his community who—through their DVDs and books—sparked a journey of reconversion in my heart. To Dorothy Day, my spirit animal, for helping me feel not quite so lonely. To all those fabulous Christian missionary women and the people who wrote their biographies: thank you for making a wandering pilgrim feminist out of me, without my ever realizing it. Thank you to Aaron Weiss and Sandra McCracken for making the soundtrack to this book. To the InnerCHANGE community, and particularly those in the exotic Midwest: I was forever changed by my time with you. Thank you for reminding me always of the commitment to celebration.

Thank you Rachelle Gardner, my agent, for helping smooth out my rough edges. To everyone at HarperOne for all of their hard work, especially Katy Hamilton. You fought for me and forced me to make my book so much better, even though I was a teensy bit difficult about it. You are a wonderful editor.

To my neighbors—well, I hardly know what to say. Through you I met Jesus—I touched him, saw him, smelled him, heard him. I will carry your stories and your ministries with me always.

This book was written over the course of four long and

tumultuous years, and I am not the same person writing this acknowledgment that I was when I wrote the first essay in this collection. In retrospect, as always, I am grateful for the ways I have been shaped and changed, although at times it felt very hard.

Most of all I offer my thanks to God, my very good Father, who can and does redeem all the ways that the world crushes us.